Jesus
Forsaken

Chiara Lubich

Jesus Forsaken

Edited by
Hubertus Blaumeiser

NEW CITY PRESS
of the Focolare
Hyde Park, NY

Published in the United States by New City Press
202 Comforter Blvd., Hyde Park, NY 12538
www.newcitypress.com
©2016 New City Press (English Translation)

Translated by Carlos Bajo and Jo-Ellen Karstens from the
original Italian *Gesù abbandonato*, by Chiara Lubich, edited by
Hubertus Blaumeiser.

©2016 Città Nuova Editrice, Rome, Italy

Cover design by Leandro De Leon and Durva Correia

Biblical citations are taken from the *New Revised Standard
Version* ©1989 Division of Christian Education of the National
Council of Churches of Christ in the United States of America.

Library of Congress Control Number 2016952566

ISBN 978-1-56548-613-3

Printed in the United States of America

Presentation of the book series*

"To those who follow you, leave only the gospel."

Chiara Lubich has articulated the gospel in many ways, which are outlined in twelve cornerstones: *God-love*, the *will of God*, the *Word of God*, love *of neighbor*, the *new commandment*, the *Eucharist*, the gift of *unity, Jesus crucified and forsaken, Mary*, the *Church-communion*, the *Holy Spirit, Jesus present among us*.

Since they emerged in the late 1940s, these points have been inscribed in the souls and in the lives of thousands of people from every corner of the earth. Nevertheless, since Chiara Lubich's death in 2008, what has been missing is a document that combined many texts, including those yet unpublished, that would illustrate them. This series of books seeks to deepen our understanding of these twelve cornerstones by presenting three sources from which they have emerged:

- the dimension of her personal testimony, especially as Chiara Lubich understood, deepened and lived these points;

- the theological dimension of reflecting on the mystery of God and of humankind;

---

* This volume contains Chiara Lubich's thought and experience on "Jesus Forsaken." While it is the eighth in this series of titles originally published in Italian by Città Nuova, it is the second to be translated in its complete form and published by New City Press. Other volumes in the series will be translated and published.

- the dimension of incarnating these points in human life via a communitarian experience, in line with Vatican II (see Lumen Gentium 9).

The series will include as many as twelve books, through which it is hoped that readers may discover:

- A great spiritual teacher who can accompany them in their spiritual life;

- A deeper appreciation of the communal aspect of Christian life, and the implications of a communitarian spirituality for the Church and humanity;

- A deeper and more personal understanding of Chiara Lubich's life and thought that they can apply in their everyday life.

Contents

3. "Like a Divine Alchemy"............................ 35

4. The Secret of Unity............................... 42

Chapter 2

The "Nothingness-Everything" of Love
Jesus Forsaken in the experience
of "Paradise '49".................................... 55

1. The Whole Gospel...
Contained in That Cry........................... 56

2. He Made Himself Sin...
To Make Everything God........................ 61

Chapter 3

"The Root of the Tree"
With Jesus Forsaken during the time

Chapter 4

"The God of Today"
  Dialogue and dedication
  to make of humanity one family 99

Chapter 5

The "Holy Journey"
Striving for Holiness,
in Communion With Others 135

Chapter 6

Introduction

It is not a trivial matter that the earthly life of Jesus culminated, according to the Gospels of Mark and Matthew, in a piercing cry: "My God, my God, why have you forsaken me?" In that question, one can find the questions, anxieties and dramas of all time. That cry opens a boundless space, and invites one to an encounter. It is far from the expression of a self-centered and overconfident person who muscles in and threatens to overwhelm the other. It is instead the cry of a God-Man who became radically poor to be within everyone's reach, a brother to everyone, thus opening a dialogue that does not exclude anyone, starting from that which defines all human experience: suffering. In fact, we have a tremendous need for dialogue in this global world in which "a piecemeal third world war" * may have already begun, and the "clash of civilizations" † is always on the horizon, while the challenges of justice and the environment are mostly ignored.

Jesus' very profound question offers an opportunity for a universal encounter. It is an opportunity of encounter with the Father who answered by raising him and exalting him, introducing him

---

* Expression coined by Pope Francis.
† The first to speak first of a "clash of civilizations" was the American political scientist Samuel P. Huntington in 1992. The term resurfaces and is deepened in an article published in 1993 in the magazine *Foreign Affairs*.

into heaven with his humanity that was battered physically, but permeated throughout with the Holy Spirit, by Love, space in which individuals and crucified peoples are welcomed and understood, and can hope for redemption.

That cry offers an opportunity for the encounter between peoples, cultures and religions in their diversity. It is no coincidence that Christianity was universal from the time of its birth at Pentecost and included a multiplicity of languages and social classes, revealing an impressive ability to assimilate into the most varied social contexts. This is because the Church has a vast openness and a limitless ability to unite, which ultimately springs out of that cry, that ultimate self-giving that breaks down all barriers and opens up infinite opportunities.

And yet it has been difficult for humanity to face that agonizing question, "Why?" It was difficult for the first Christians to proclaim the cross, because it was a clear sign of disgrace, of a curse. Augustine of Hippo affirmed that Jesus uttered that cry on our behalf, giving voice to our state of perdition. This was the prevalent thinking for nearly two millennia, with the exception of some mystics who, experiencing moments of the "dark night," penetrated into that mystery. Among these, St. John of the Cross writes: "It is certain that, at the moment of his death, he was likewise annihilated in his soul, and was deprived of any relief and consolation, since his Father left him in the most intense aridity [...]. Wherefore he had perforce to cry out, saying: 'My God, my God, why have you forsaken me?' (Mt 27:46). This was the greatest desolation that he had suffered in his life. And thus he wrought herein the greatest work that he had ever wrought, whether in miracles or in mighty works, during the whole of his life, either upon earth or in heaven, which was the reconciliation and union of mankind, through grace, with God." *

It was not until the twentieth century, wounded by the extermination camps and the gulags, gripped by atheism and extreme doubt, with a new awareness of the cry of the poor that rises from all over the earth, that theologians began to explore more deeply the meaning of that cry.†

Martin Heidegger, reflecting on the "death of God" proclaimed by Nietzsche, wrote about this troubled century: "The night of the world spreads its darkness. This era is characterized by the absence of God, the 'disappearance of God.' [...] Granted that there can be a turning point for this age, this can only happen if the world turns upside down, that is, upside down beginning from the abyss. In an epoch of the world's dark night, the abyss must be experienced and suffered. But for this to happen, it is necessary that there are those who reach into the abyss." ‡

Jesus on the cross, abandoned by the one whom he had called "Abba, Father," and thrust into the blackest night, tells us that at least he has reached into the abyss. Of course, there were those who

---

* *Ascent of Mount Carmel*, 2, 7, 11, in Opere, Roma 1979, 92.
† For a deeper analysis, see the Forum, *Jesus' abandonment, for a culture of unity*, in *Nuova Umanita* with articles by Giuseppe Maria Zanghi, Gerard Rosee, Piero Coda and Jesus Castellano Cervera, OCD.
‡ *Sentieri interrotti*, ed. it., Firenze 1982, 247–248.

believed, throughout history, that his "why have you forsaken me?" was nothing more than a verse from Psalm 22, recited by him as a dying prayer. But Biblical science tells us that those words are not randomly inserted in the story of Christ's passion, but rather express its deepest meaning: Jesus did not remain a stranger to disgrace, but he experienced the abyss of nothingness and descended into the state of extreme remoteness from God.

Paul confirms this in his Letter to the Galatians when he does not hesitate to say that Christ was made "a curse for us," * and when, in Second Corinthians, he affirms that God "made him to be sin." † Similarly, the Letter to the Hebrews declares that Jesus died "outside the camp," that is, outside the enclosure of the Holy City and the scope of the Covenant: in the space of those without God (cf. Heb 13:12–13). ‡

Great theologians of different churches have reflected on this reality. The Catholic theologian, Hans Urs von Balthasar, writes: "Jesus does experience the darkness of the sinful state, not in the same way as the (God-hating) sinner experiences it [...], but nonetheless in a deeper and darker experience. This is because it takes place in the profound

---

*   Cf Gal 3:13 "Cursed be everyone who hangs on a tree." Cf. Deut 21:23 "hanging on a cross is a curse from God." When death on the cross, Gerard Rosse observes, was inflicted in the name of the Law, it meant, based on Scripture, an act of repulsion and abandonment by God.

†   Cf. 2 Cor 5:21: "For our sake he made him to be sin who did not know sin, so that we might become the righteousness of God in him."

‡   Cf. G. Rosse, *Maledetto l'appeso al legno. Lo scandalo della croce in Paolo e Marco*, Roma 2006.

depths of the relations between the divine *hypostases,* which is inconceivable to any creature. Thus it is just as possible to maintain that Jesus' being forsaken by God was the opposite of hell, as to say that it was hell or even the ultimate heightening of hell." *

In Orthodox circles, Sergei Bulgakov writes this about the abandonment of Jesus: "It is as if the inseparability of the Holy Trinity is disrupted; the Son is alone, and by this astonishing sacrifice of God, the 'it is finished' of the salvation of the world arrives. This is the divine death, for 'my soul is exceeding sorrowful, even unto death;' this is spiritual death, which is precisely forsakenness by God. The cup is drunk to the bottom and the Son commends his Spirit into the Father's hands. The Divine Trinity is reunited into an inseparable unity." †

In the Evangelical Lutheran perspective, Luther, distancing himself from Augustine, had already reiterated that the cry of Jesus was to be taken literally and not attenuated in its shocking reality. Theologians like Karl Barth and Dietrich Bonhoeffer have also reflected deeply on the subject.

In the official teaching of the Catholic Church, John Paul II was the first to speak of Jesus' cry of abandonment reported by the evangelists. He writes in the apostolic letter *Salvifici Doloris*: "One can say that these words on abandonment are born at the level of that inseparable union of the Son

---

*   *Teodrammatica*, IV, Milano 1986, 313.
†   Sergej Bulkakov, *L'Agnello di Dio*, Città Nuova, Rome, 1986, 433.

with the Father, and are born because the Father 'laid on him the iniquity of us all' (Is 53:6). They also foreshadow the words of Saint Paul: 'For our sake he made him to be sin who knew no sin' (2 Cor 5:21). Together with this horrible weight, encompassing the 'entire' evil of the turning away from God which is contained in sin, Christ, through the divine depth of his filial union with the Father, perceives in a humanly inexpressible way this suffering which is the separation, the rejection by the Father, the estrangement from God. But precisely through this suffering he accomplishes the Redemption, and can say as he breathes his last: 'It is finished' (John 19:30)" (n. 18)*

The Ecumenical Patriarch of Constantinople, Bartholomew, writes: "Jesus, the Word made flesh, has gone the farthest distance that a lost humanity is able to go. 'My God, my God, why have you forsaken me?' Endless distance, limitless separation, wonder of love. Between God and God, between the Father and his Incarnate Son, our despair intervenes, with which Jesus shows solidarity until the end."†

Pope Francis spoke of the cry of abandonment in a spontaneous answer to young people: "But the greatest silence of God was on the cross: Jesus felt the Father's silence, calling it 'abandonment.' 'Father, why have you abandoned me?' And then there was the miracle of God, that word, that magnificent gesture which was the Resurrection. Our

---

* John Paul II spoke again about Jesus' abandonment in his Apostolic Letter *Novo millennio ineunte*, 25–27.

† Via Crucis at the Colosseum, Rome, April 1, 1994.

God is also a God of silences and [...] I am not saying that we can 'understand' the silences of God, but we can come close to them by looking at Christ crucified, Christ who died, Christ abandoned..." *

But how could the Son of God feel abandoned by the Father? How could the Father abandon the Son?

This is the mystery that Chiara Lubich encountered at the age of twenty-four on January 24, 1944. Her conclusion was disarming: "If at that moment he suffered the most, it means that at that moment he loved the most. Let's make him the Ideal of our lives! Let's go look for him and 'console' him wherever he is suffering—in any suffering. Let's not run away from him but 'embrace' him in the many crosses of ours and other people's lives. And let's gather for him hearts that also start loving him."

Far from a painful and sorrowful Christianity, this is a love story, full of surprises. This choice, carried out little by little, without reservations, brought forth light. Chiara first discovered the key to unity in Jesus Forsaken; then the "pupil of the Eye of God" through which he sees us and we can "see" him—a new vision of God and of all things. Finally, she recognized in the abandonment the intimate wound of the God-Man from which emanated the Holy Spirit who later, at Pentecost, descended on the newborn Church. It follows that he is really the secret of unity and the road to become an instrument of unity on a universal scale.

---

*   Meeting with youth at Lungomare Caracciolo, Naples, March 21, 2015.

The consequences of these findings were multiple. Initially, they indicated to Chiara the challenging road to graft a dazzling and innovative charism into the Church, whose leaders did not immediately understand it, and to bring about a Work that is *Church*, a creature of the Church. Then, Jesus Forsaken became the reason to "go out" to face the most varied challenges of society and recognize his face on a grand scale, arousing love for him, who when lived, as much as possible with his measure, is a remedy and a response. Jesus Forsaken invited us to take upon ourselves any rift, laceration or division, patiently weaving a dialogue with others, without excluding anyone, including ecumenical and interreligious dialogue, as well as dialogue with non-believers and with all the various expressions of contemporary culture.

This is precisely how Chiara discovered Jesus Forsaken—"God who empties himself," as Pope Francis says, referring to the words of Paul in Phil 2:7. Chiara sees him as the "God of today," "the God of our time," not the God of exclamation points, much less the God of imposition, but the God who welcomes, listens to, serves and takes upon himself every burden. Therefore, he is the God of people who do not hide behind their own security, but give of themselves to others, dare to make room for them, and build bridges in all directions in order to promote fraternity.

Finally, with Jesus Forsaken, Chiara descended into the "epochal night," the collective dark night, as John Paul II clearly diagnosed it, and she lived it, in her own flesh, as the "night of God," shoulder to shoulder with millions of people living in the most unspeakable situations, as an indispensable step to spread what she one day called the "culture of the resurrection."

Chiara spoke and "sang" of all this in her book *The Cry* published in 2000. She also recounted it with passion in the early 80s in the book, *Unity and Jesus Forsaken*. In the following pages, we retrace this path through letters of the "early days," various little-known writings scattered in publications not easily accessible, meditations, journal notes, excerpts taken from talks directed to different audiences and from spiritual thoughts given during international conference calls, which initially occurred fortnightly and then monthly, and through which Chiara carried on, with tens of thousands of people all over the world, what she called the "Holy Journey." *

Through these first-hand testimonies, we will revisit the life and thought of Chiara from a particular perspective that is one of the main points of her spirituality,† actually one of its two main pillars, together with unity.

In chapter after chapter we will see a great love story unfold, increasingly far-reaching. The result will be an invitation to us to respond also to the cry

---

* A heartfelt thanks to the Chiara Lubich Center and to the many people who in different ways contributed to this book, which would not have been possible without them.

† This series of books is dedicated to the main points of the spirituality of unity, which Chiara also called "spirituality of communion," in line with John Paul II's thought expressed in his apostolic Letter *Novo millenio ineunte* (cf. n. 43).

that bursts from within the God-Man and rises up globally from humankind. A cry that invokes love.

And since that cry embraces everyone, we conclude this introduction with the words attributed to the Muslim poet Saadi, who lived in thirteenth-century Persia:

"When I came into the world,
life handed me a cup:
I drank it all and found a pearl, youth.
Youth gave me its cup
and after drinking from it
I found between my lips the ruby of love.
Love offered me its cup, I drank also from it,
and at the bottom there was the diamond of
    pain.
Desperate, I drank to the last drop
from the cup of pain,
and with great amazement, I found God."

Hubertus Blaumeiser

"My God, my God, why have you forsaken me?"

"When it was noon, darkness came over the whole
land until three in the afternoon.
At three o'clock Jesus cried out with a loud voice,
'Eloi, Eloi, lema sabachthani?' which means,
'My God, my God, why have you forsaken me?'
When some of the bystanders heard it, they said,
'Listen, he is calling for Elijah.'
And someone ran, filled a sponge with sour wine,
put it on a stick, and gave it to him to drink,
saying,
'Wait, let us see whether Elijah will come to take
him down.'
Then Jesus gave a loud cry and breathed his last.
And the curtain of the temple was torn in two,
from top to bottom.
Now when the centurion, who stood facing him,
saw that in this way he breathed his last, he said,
'Truly this man was God's Son!'"

Mk 15:33–39

Io me solo sono sulla terra: Perché Abbandonato: non ho altro Dio fuori di Lui. In Lui è tutto il Paradiso colla Trinità e tutta la terra coll'Umanità.

Perciò il suo è mio e null'altro.

E Suo è il Dolore universale e quindi mio.

Andrò pel mondo cercandoLo sino qui ultimo della mia vita.

Ciò che mi fa male è mio.

Mio il dolore che mi sfiora nel presente. Mio il dolore delle anime accanto (è quello il mio Perù). Mio tuttociò che non è pace, gaudio, bello, amabile, sereno... in una parola: ciò che non è Paradiso. Perché solo io ho il mio Paradiso ma è quello nel cuore dello Sposo mio. Non ne voglio altri. Così per gli anni che mi rimangono: assetata di dolori, di angoscie, di disperazioni, di malinconie, di distacchi, di esilio, di abbandoni, di strazi, di ... tuttociò che è Lui e Lui è il Peccato, l'Inferno.

Così prosciugherò l'acqua della tribolazione in molti cuori vicini e per la comu=

nione colla Sposo mio onnipotente - lontani:

Passerò come Fuoco che consuma ciò che ha da cadere e lascia in piedi solo la Verità.

Ma occorre esser come Lui: esser Lui nel momento presente della vita.

I have only one Spouse on earth

The text presented in this page is one of Chiara Lubich's most famous writings: a love letter to Jesus Forsaken, composed after the extraordinary experience of God and of his Light during the summer of 1949. It is a lifetime program.

September 20, 1949[1]

I have only one Spouse on earth: Jesus Forsaken. I have no other God but him.

In him there is the whole of paradise with the Trinity and the whole of the earth with Humanity.

Therefore what is his is mine, and nothing else.

And his is universal Pain, and therefore mine.

I will go through the world seeking him in every instant of my life.

What hurts me is *mine*.

Mine the pain that grazes me in the present. Mine the pain of the souls beside me (that is my Jesus).

Mine all that is not peace, joy, beautiful, lovable, serene...in a word, what is not Paradise. Because I too have my Paradise, but it is that in my Spouse's heart. I know no other.

So it will be for the years I have left: athirst for pain, for anguish, for despair, for sadness, for separation, for exile, for forsakenness, for torment, for...all that is him, and he is Sin, Hell.

In this way I will dry up the waters of tribulation in many hearts nearby and, through communion with my almighty Spouse, in many far away.

I shall pass as a Fire that consumes all that must fall and leaves standing only the Truth. But it is necessary to be *like* him: to be him in the present moment of life.

To Reunite Us All With the Father

Taken from "A Little Harmless Manifesto"

Trent, 1950[2]

We knew Christ Crucified and nothing else.

To be crucified with him in the divine will and often with him crucified in our neighbor was the most beautiful expression of our love for the Father. "So that the world may believe..." (Jn 17:21)

We fixed our gaze on him and realized that the great saints filled their souls with God by loving the cross. We wanted to do the same. We knew we had only one life, and a brief one at that, so we wanted to spend it in the best possible way.

One day we asked ourselves what was the greatest suffering of Jesus on the cross and it seemed to us that it was that cry, uttered after three hours of agony, "My God, my God, why have you forsaken me?" (cf Mt 27:46; Mk 15:34). It is like the swan song of the God-Man who had poured out everything of himself for his brothers and sisters.

He had given everything.

First, a life lived beside Mary in hardship, obedience and dedication.

Then three years of mission, revealing the Truth, giving witness to the Father, promising the Holy Spirit, and working all kinds of miracles of love.

Finally, three hours on the cross, from which he gave forgiveness to his executioners, opened paradise to the thief, gave his mother to us, and ultimately gave his body and blood, after having given them mystically in the Eucharist.

He had nothing left but his divinity, his union with the Father, that sweet and ineffable union with the One who had made him so powerful on earth as the Son of God and so regal on the cross. That feeling of God's presence had to disappear from the depths of his soul and no longer make itself felt, separating him somehow from the One with whom he had claimed to be one: "The Father and I are one" (Jn 10:30). In him, love was annihilated, the light extinguished, wisdom silenced.

He totally committed himself to humanity, making himself sin with sinners. He had signed a check of infinite value, which no one could pay but him. Now the Father was permitting this darkness and infinite aridity of the soul, this infinite nothingness, to make him feel "cursed" by heaven and by earth. Jesus paid for us. To make us children of God he deprived himself of the feeling of being the Son of God.

We were separated from the Father. It was necessary that the Son, who represented all of us as words in the Word and as flesh of his divine flesh, would experience being separated from the Father in order to reunite us all to the Father. "For through him God was pleased to reconcile to himself all things, whether on earth or in heaven, by making peace through the blood of his cross." (Col 1:20).

It was the peak of utmost suffering, the night of the senses, the dark night of the soul, the apparent abandonment of God, which he had to experience so that no human being would ever feel abandoned again.

He had taught that there is no greater love than one who lays down their life for their friends. He, Life, gave everything of himself.

This is the apex of his passion. In that moment, he is the Redeemer. He is the most beautiful expression of Love.

He loves as God, with a love that is greater than God himself. He makes himself nothing to make us everything. He makes himself "us," in order to transform us into him, into children of God.

He was beautiful, oh, so beautiful, this divine lover of our souls. He was rejected by heaven and by earth, disdained by everyone, even repulsive, reduced to shame, in order to introduce us into the kingdom as children of God, co-heirs with him, welcomed by everyone, full of his light, his love, his power, overflowing with honor and dignity. "He emptied himself..." (Phil 2:7)

We loved him like this, we wanted him like this. Never as in that moment did he appear as God, the God of Love, who gives everything of himself.

And from him burst forth, as if from a divine treasure chest, jewels of light and strength for all those who followed him.

We saw him everywhere, in every person who was suffering. Every physical, moral or spiritual pain seemed to be a reflection of his immense suffering.

Everything we personally suffered appeared to us as an aspect of Jesus Crucified to be loved and desired. We wanted to be like him, so that, through the death of ourselves, loved and desired, Life would be given to ourselves and to many other people.

Every painful event was a countenance of his that we embraced so as to be one with him—abandoned with him who was abandoned, darkness and boredom and cold and aridity and desperation and detachment and anguish and hunger and pain...to be with him who personified every suffering.

And yet, underlying all of these painful aspects of life, we found him, the one true God, perfect peace, fullness of joy, the light...all things that are not of this world.

Even among those who had taken God as their Ideal, and had decided to put him first in their lives, there were those who gave up. The Lord permits big trials when he gives big graces and the first small group of people felt the shock of those who left them.

Without unity there was death, just as in unity we had Life.

And yet the antidote to death was Jesus Crucified and Forsaken.

When those who lived in the focolare house felt crushed because of being abandoned by a brother or sister, they understood that in that moment they were similar to Jesus and would make the effort to be glad of their pain since they had chosen Jesus Forsaken as their one and only love. But not only, they saw in the other person, who was disunited, another Jesus Forsaken to be consoled, to be loved. And love re-established unity.

While we gradually came to understand more deeply this Ideal [the new spirituality of unity], especially the mystery of unity brought about by Jesus on the cross, many, very many people were attracted to the light and love that emanated from our group.

Chapter 1

"A Hidden, Unknown Wound"
Jesus Forsaken in the letters
of the "early days"

The discovery of Jesus' cry of abandonment on the cross as his greatest suffering came to Chiara unexpectedly, a few weeks after December 7, 1943, when she "espoused God," giving her whole self to him forever. Jesus had not only suffered the rejection and the torment of the cross inflicted by human hands, but had also experienced the silence of God. Chiara's answer was immediate: "If Jesus' greatest pain was his abandonment by his Father, we will choose him as our Ideal and that is the way we will follow him."[3]

Doriana Zamboni, who was an eyewitness of that discovery, recounted: "From that day on, Chiara spoke to me often, in fact constantly, about Jesus Forsaken. He was the living personality in our lives."[4] Thus began a love story that, in a steady crescendo, was the fulcrum of Chiara's whole life and drew along countless people throughout the world.[5] Choosing Jesus Forsaken was a choice of love, without any

ulterior motive, not even related—as it happened in the case of other great Christian
figures—to particular trials. In a completely
unexpected way, he soon revealed his Risen
face that transforms suffering into love and allows every wounded relationship with God and
among people to become the beginning of a
path to unity. We retrace here these discoveries,
as reflected in the letters of those early years
in which Chiara's charism came to light.[6] They
are words, and above all experiences, which
resonate, even today, as an invitation to re-live
them in order to love Love and contribute to
the unity of the human family.

1. "Love Reappeared in the World"

The discovery of Jesus Forsaken on January
24, 1944, is often recounted in later writings.
The letters of the early years show instead how
the encounter with him brought forth "a blaz-
ing Love," "which eclipsed any other reality."

The first time I spoke of him

From a talk given in Rocca di Papa, Italy

December 7, 1971[7]

First, an episode preceding our history.

The first focolare house did not exist yet; I had
not yet met my first companion. I was a teacher,
and one day a very zealous person approached me.
She was running a youth group and had succeeded
in attracting the youth to religion through recre-

ation, music, and story telling. She asked if I could speak to them, and I said yes.

"What will you speak about?" she asked. "Love," I said. "What is love?" she went on, interested. "Jesus Crucified," I answered.

This may have been the very first time in my life, when not yet a focolarina,* that I spoke of him.

In those days, even in traditionally religious environments like the ones we came from, it was uncommon to hear anyone speaking about love; and even less, to believe that the Crucified One, who draws all to himself, was a valid means for the apostolate of our times.

Nevertheless, I admit that to this day I do not know who put on my lips that definition of love.

Later on, I understood that Jesus Crucified (Paul said it, too) "gave himself for us" (Eph 5:2), "gave himself for me" (Gal 2:20).

The one who preceded every other reality

From a talk given in Rocca di Papa, Italy

December 23, 1983[8]

We feel urged by a legitimate desire, but also by the Church's advice, which invites religious families and movements to return to the times when the Holy Spirit gave them life. If we look at

---

* Focolarine (women) and focolarini (men) are members who are consecrated in the Focolare in order to spread the spirit of unity. The singular for men is focolarino and for women is focolarina.

the beginnings of the movement, we can see that before having those ideas about how to accomplish unity, a model, a figure, a life, was presented to us.

It was the life of the One who truly knew how to make himself one with all people who were, who are and who will be; the One who brought about unity, paying for it with the cross, with his blood and his cry of abandonment; the One who gave the Church his presence as the Risen Lord for all time, until the end of the world—Jesus Crucified and Forsaken. The reality of Jesus Forsaken, and our understanding of who he is, preceded every other idea, also in time.

The greatest suffering of all

From a talk given in Rocca di Papa, Italy

December 7, 1971[9]

How did it happen that Jesus Forsaken showed himself to us as our specific vocation?

It was January 24, 1944, when a priest told us that Jesus' greatest suffering was in the moment he cried out on the cross: "My God, my God, why have you forsaken me?" (Mt 27:46; Mk 15:34).

The most commonly held opinion among Christians at that time was that the greatest suffering of Jesus took place in Gethsemane. And yet we had great faith in the words of the priest, because he was God's minister, and so we believed that the suffering of the abandonment was the greatest.

On the other hand, we know that this conviction is also now becoming common patrimony in the fields of theology and spirituality.

The meeting with that priest, although an external circumstance, was, as we can see now, God's response to our prayer. Fascinated by the beauty of Jesus' testament, we first focolarine, all united, had asked him, in his name, to teach us how to bring about the unity he had asked of the Father before he died—in the way he saw it should be.[10]

During these almost fifty-six years of life in the movement, we have always experienced that what makes unity possible is exactly this love for Jesus Crucified and Forsaken.

The circumstance mentioned above, moreover, carried a message for us. Jesus Forsaken was making himself known to us for the first time, so that we could choose him, or better, so that he could choose us, inviting us to become his disciples. As he said: "You did not choose me, but I chose you" (Jn 15:16).

He had placed himself at the head of all the many people who, together with us, have followed him, follow him today and will follow him in the future. We had no doubts about this. His call was strong and decisive. Jesus Forsaken very soon became everything for us.

The proof of our love for him
From a letter to Elena Molignoni

June 7, 1944[11]

It is true that I studied at the university, but no book, however beautiful or profound, has given such strength to my soul and, above all, such love, as has Jesus Crucified.

Before him, every suffering seems like nothing to me and I await suffering, large or small, *as the greatest gift of God*, since this is the proof of my love for him!

My dear Elena, I beg you, and I would write this with my blood: love the Crucified Lord! It's all summed up there, the whole gift of God. He couldn't give us anything more.

And when you feel some big or small pain, cry out with me: "Thank you! Oh, thank you, my Immense Love! I don't only accept what you give me but I offer it to you with supreme joy. I give you all the love I have in my heart!"

Just think, Elena, *we can love God with this little heart of ours!* We can love *God!* Oh, no one will ever take this love away from us, not even the worst bombardments. (...)

May the Lord take everything from you and give you only a great Love, a Love of fire, of flames.

With our soul inside the wound of the abandonment

From a letter to Rosetta Zanoni

December 8, 1944[12]

Do you know Jesus Forsaken? Do you realize that he gave us everything? What more could he give us—a God who, out of love, seems to forget that he is God?

We, who with you, are following this most beautiful and fascinating Ideal, have thrown our whole soul into the new wound of the Abandonment! And in there we are safe because we live in the Heart of our Love. Not only, but from within that wound we can see the Immensity of God's Love poured out over the world.

Place yourself inside, too! You'll have the Light of Love, because Jesus is the Light of the world.

You don't know your good fortune, and ours, to be able to follow this forsaken Love!

In his inscrutable designs, he chose us among thousands and thousands, among millions of people, to let us hear his cry of anguish: "My God, my God, why have you forsaken me?"

And, as God, he's made this cry *into the rule of a new life, following a new Ideal.*

So that Love is not abandoned

From a letter to Duccia Calderari[13]

Advent 1944[14]

Believe me, Duccia, *Love* is going to be the salvation of the 20th century because *Love* is God. All the more or less secular traps are a waste of time or perhaps they serve as the subsoil for God's plans.

Fill yourself, then, with this personal Love for the God-Man, the only one who is truly worthy of love. [...] And Love *has* reappeared in the world and given to our hearts the *Key* that opens *every* heart.

Believe it, Duccia, everyone who rose to holiness was given a more or less lofty place relative to the amount of intensity with which they *loved Jesus Crucified*! And so, do what I want to do, too: plunge yourself, body and soul, *into the Abandoned Love*!

You have a heart and you can understand, so listen to me.

Think of the infinite difference between the pain of Jesus, who was crucified by his *enemies*, abandoned by his disciples, forced to entrust his Mother to another, and the immense pain of feeling separated from his Father whom he loved as himself and with whom he formed a single oneness.

Think about it! It was that atrocious doubt of no longer being one with the Father that made him burst out with that cry: "My God, my God why have you forsaken me?"

This cry should break the heart of every man and woman, because it was by this divine anguish that every human being has been made worthy of being *joined* to God, *united* to God as an adopted child!

There, right there, is the *Immensity of Love*! He gives us his Divinity.

Just think, Duccia, you who have such a big heart, think of Jesus hanging there like a rag, his soul torn by grief, *doubting whether he's still God!*

Think of it and let him rest on that heart of yours that desires great things, but great things through him! [...]

Swear to him, assure him with your life that he *is God* precisely because, out of Love, he desired to remain in doubt for that moment!

Swear to him that your heart will never again abandon him, so that he can always find in your heart the paradise that he lost when it seemed his Father had turned his eyes away.

And then do whatever you want, for it will all be great in the eyes of God and of the world. [...]

Don't slow down, Duccia, and with that generosity that blossoms so easily within you, put yourself at the disposal of God's plans. Be strong and make the decision, almost like an oath, and promise him that, as long as you are alive, you will do everything possible so that *Love will never be abandoned* by you or by anyone else.

But you won't be able to do it unless you sincerely love him and don't spare anything in Love for him.

2. "Run Through the World to Gather Hearts for Him"

The discovery of the greatest suffering-love brings forth immediately in Chiara a passion to attract as many people as possible to the adventure of answering to the Forsaken's love. I would like "to run through the world to gather hearts for him. And I feel that all the hearts of the world would never be enough for a love as great as God," she wrote in 1948 to a religious priest.[15] This burning desire had already been present from the very first months after this discovery.

Jesus transformed the world with the testimony of his Love

From a letter to Rosetta Zanoni

November 1944[16]

Think of it, Rosetta, God came to earth only once, and that one time, he became a man *and let himself be put on the cross!* This thought gives me great strength to accept with joy the small crosses that are always with us.

But when he gives some bigger suffering to the souls that he loves, *like yours, which has been touched by Love, it's because he wants his Love to triumph in you completely!*

[...] But the person *who knows Love and unites his or her sufferings to those of Jesus on the cross, drowning their own drop* of blood into that ocean of blood of the Divine Blood of Christ, has the *highest place of honor that a person can have: to be like God who came into the world, the Redeemer of the world.*

Rosetta, you are *with us!* Your love for the Lord is totally one with our love for him.

Oh! I beg you with my whole heart: Don't let even a moment of your precious life be lost by spending it in vain.

Do you know what I mean? Oh, yes, you know! Jesus converted the world with the word, his example and his preaching, but he transformed it *with the proof of his Love: the cross.*

Hanging there for two and a half hours in a state of such tremendous anguish and horrendous pain, he drew all hearts to himself.

Believe me, Rosetta: one minute of your life on that sickbed—if you accept the gift of God with joy—is worth more than all the activity of a preacher who speaks and speaks and loves God very little.

You will see that all the rest will be given to you as well

From a letter to her mother

December 1944[17]

Believe it, Mom! Jesus died for you and being God, he would have died for you alone if that had been necessary for your salvation!

Look at him there, crucified, and think: What if it had been your son? Listen to him cry out, "My God, my God, why have you forsaken me?"

It's a cry that echoes every moment in my heart. Think of him dying, nearly desperate, and pierced like a lamb! Poor Jesus! Come on, Mom, tell me that you love him, too, and that you want to make others love him! Tell me that if your Sylvia[18] had to die before you, you would take as your own the flame that burns in her heart.

I've experienced something of this world, too, Mom, and I've found hearts that were more or less noble, but I've found no one who loves me as much as he does.

In heaven you will know how much he's forgiven me and also the marvels he is working in me and in the young women who are following my way, the way of Love.

Don't tell anything to anyone, Mom!

I've married him and I've tried to extinguish every other desire for him. He and his Cry of Abandonment have swept me away, Mom, and made me pass over everything else, with a heart that is broken. Yes, Mom, only he could have done it. [...]

Yes, yes, everything, even death, as long as Jesus who loved us so much as to die for us is loved by all people, as long as he receives consolation and there is peace in the hearts of those who don't have any other expectations but to love Love! You'll see, Mom, how all the rest will be given to you as well, when we seek only his kingdom! And what is his kingdom if not telling everyone to love the Lord God and to love each other?

He draws hearts along to follow him
From a letter to Pierita Folgheraiter

Christmas 1944[19]

Oh, my little Pierinetta, how I'd like to have you near to me at this time of hard and bitter struggle: *but also of so much Light and Fire and Warmth!* You know what's happened to me externally; you're up to date on my sufferings which have certainly opened my heart to an understanding of what humanity suffers; but you don't know, you don't know what this suffering has given to me. [...]

You know that Jesus, my Jesus and yours, has made me suffer. And I have suffered! But he is not a distributor of pain! No, no! He *permits* it, always, but never *sends* the suffering that *people are always causing* for themselves. He distributes *only Love!*

He can only Love! He draws hearts to follow him: he is all and only Love!

No one knows how to love like him! No one knows how to console like him! He has infused a great passion within my heart: Jesus Crucified and Forsaken!

From high on the cross, he tells me: "Everything that was mine I have extinguished for you—everything! I am no longer beautiful, no longer strong; here I have no more peace; up here, justice is dead; knowledge is unknown; truth disappears. All that remains is my Love, which wants to pour out all my riches as God *for you*...." That's how he speaks to me and he calls me with his passionate love to follow him, as one who is "madly in love."

[...]

May Love make you understand how much he has loved you, and loves you. And may he give your heart my Passion of Love, so that, in you, too, he may finally find on earth a small heart that will give him some consolation, which the world denies him.

Live him in the moment that passes

From a letter to a focolarino at the end of 1949[20]

I would like to be near you to tell you always, "Walk in the light if you are a child of the light." But since I cannot be there, I give you my Spouse.

Open wide your heart and welcome my Forsaken Love.

He is my Spouse and yours. Live him in the moment that passes. He is the Light of the world, the Victory in every battle, Peace in every anguish, the Source of God, infinite and most pure Love, the Medicine for every evil, the best Consoler.

All and only what is mine is there; and only there, with the Spouse, will you find your mother.

3. "Like a Divine Alchemy"

"Throw yourself into a sea of pain and you find yourself swimming in an ocean of love, of perfect joy," [21] is the surprising observation that Chiara increasingly made, after months and months in which she tried only to love and "console" the Forsaken Love. In fact, Jesus Crucified and Forsaken is also inseparably the Risen One.

In light of her experience, Chiara explains what is necessary so that we can experience this "divine alchemy." It means recognizing in any pain—without stopping to analyze it—the face of Jesus in his abandonment. It requires "embracing" him, uniting ourselves to him and, with him, entrusting ourselves completely to the Father. Then we need to plunge into living the will of God in the present moment and in giving ourselves to others, and the life of the Risen Lord will gradually shine out in us. Chiara wrote: "I wish to bear witness before the world that Jesus Forsaken has filled every void, illuminated every darkness, accompanied every solitude, annulled every suffering, cancelled out every sin." [22]

The fullness of joy

In a talk in 2005, Chiara spoke about her letters from the "early days" [23]

From the very first days of our movement, one of the characteristic fruits of living the charism was the divine alchemy that changes suffering into love and makes the soul experience the presence of God beyond suffering.

We definitely felt that we could not remain in the suffering and we were convinced that with the Ideal of unity we had the grace to live, in our ordinary life, the fullness of joy promised by Jesus.

We could not conceive of a love for Jesus Forsaken that did not blossom, sooner or later, in the resurrection.

All that is mine is yours

From a letter to Fosca Pellegrini

Second Sunday of Easter, April 15, 1945[24]
Our soul is either in joy or it is in sorrow.

When the soul doesn't sing, then something is preoccupying it and this something should immediately be given to God.

The suffering could be brought on by external things (and these are more easily overcome by souls who want to love Love); the sufferings could be within us (scruples, doubts, melancholy, temptations, emptiness, homesickness).

They all need to be given to God.

The quicker the giving, the sooner Love descends into our hearts.

But be careful! Remember that the person who gives cannot keep for themselves the gift that's been given away.

If you feel something, *whatever it may be*, which doesn't allow your soul to be at peace, then you need to give it over to him with an effort that is equal to the size of the gift.

If you keep something for yourself, even just the thought of the gift, then you appropriate a treasure for yourself (a miserable treasure) that no longer belongs to you.

Besides, it is only into the extreme poverty of a soul that loses itself out of love that *the Lord God will enter triumphant, with the fullness of joy.*

That is why this Easter was a "passing over" for all of us to a life of never-ending joy, as long as we live the Ideal in its fullness.

Do you want to know our Eternal Model?

It is Jesus Crucified and Forsaken.

His soul, which is the soul of the God-Man, filled with the greatest suffering ever known in heaven and on earth, the suffering of a God abandoned by God, never doubted for a moment about offering it to his Father: "Into your hands, Lord, I commend my spirit." [25]

Let it always be the same for us.

And do you know what Jesus will say in answer to your offering?

"All that is mine is yours." [26]

He'll give you *everything*, all the fullness of his joy.

Love that makes fear disappear

From a letter to her mother

August 1946[27]

Be courageous and close the eyes of your heart that is so rebellious and of your human nature that resists, and go beyond everything! Embrace the Cross!

As soon as you embrace it, you will realize... that you have found him! Then you will unite your wounded soul to his and you will be filled with such sweetness that every bitterness will be overcome, with such love that every suffering will disappear!

Jesus can only be found there: *on the cross!* And it's on the cross that he accepts us!

But who understands him? Who takes care of him?

At least you, you who know this, at least you! Don't let him escape you.

When he cuts you to the quick, it's because he wants to unite you to himself crucified!

And so, *forget everything* in order to look for him!

Love the Cross if you want to love him.

That's the only true Resurrection! Only in it do we have every hope!

To give us a life of happiness on earth

From the writings of 1949–1951

Summer 1950[28]

I would die if I did not look at you, my Love, you who transform, as if by magic, every bitterness into sweetness—at you, upon the cross in your Cry and mine, in the highest suspense, in absolute inactivity, in living death, when, made cold, you threw all your Fire on the earth and, made infinite stillness, you cast your infinite life to us, who now live it with fullness and in elation.

And this is enough for me: seeing myself like you, at least a little, and uniting my pain to yours and offering it to the Father and remaining certain that never—as in these hours—does so much Light travel through this world, and so much Fire.

So that we might have Light, you made yourself blind.

So that we might have union, you tasted separation from the Father.

So that we might possess Wisdom, you made yourself "ignorance."

So that we might be clothed with innocence, you became "sin."

So that we might have hope, you almost despaired...

So that God might be in us, you felt him far from you.

So that Heaven might be ours, you experienced Hell.

So that we might have a glad sojourn on earth, among hundreds of brothers and sisters, you were banished from Heaven and from earth, from humankind and from nature.

You are God, you are my God, *our* God of infinite love.

Rome, November 23, 1950[29]

There are some souls who live Jesus Forsaken, but not as he would wish to be loved. They are always in Jesus Forsaken and never pass on to be *Jesus*.

Jesus Forsaken is a passage and is to be passed through.

Jesus Forsaken is like a factory making Jesus, like a machine that forms Jesuses. It is necessary for us to *come out Jesus*, not stay stuck in the machine.

I found the hidden treasure

A text that covers the first steps in the discovery of Jesus Forsaken

February 24, 1957[30]

Do you remember, Jesus, when I was a young woman and I asked you that I might penetrate into your suffering, and I looked for your wounds as a way to enter your heart? I wanted to discover the mystery of your passion and so I asked you, "Give me the passion for your passion!"

How impenetrable was your suffering!

How inaccessible it was for my heart. But you heard my prayer and my desire, which you yourself had put in me, and you started to work, allowing me to taste your own pains.

At first, you let me discover that there is an unknown, hidden wound in your heart, one that had never been discovered, a wound that is all spiritual, compared to which the wound in your side was nothing. It was the wound of the abandonment—the terrible trauma of your soul.

Then, little by little, you allowed me to penetrate into your suffering, your infinite suffering! And, something unheard of, beyond the door that spoke to me of death and infinite anguish, I found love, and all suffering disappeared.

I found the law of life.

Jesus, you know what I am saying.

Whoever enters into your infinite pain finds, as if by magic, everything transformed into love. God lies beneath that veil of infinite desperation and in him is the created universe and the uncreated heaven.

I found the hidden treasure, every science, every beauty, every goodness, every love. I found life.

Only you, Jesus, know what I found there.

Jesus, my beautiful Jesus, where is your great pain?

I knew that everything was all love, but I would have never imagined it to be like this.

Jesus Forsaken is the man who becomes God.

Suffering is not, Love is. God is—and nothing else except what has to become him. Dying out of love is love.

And in love there is Light and Life.

Who will understand me? Jesus, you understand me because I am in you and you are in me. And those who are with me are also in you.

Give me the grace to love you as you love me.

4. The Secret of Unity

The unity invoked by Jesus in the prayer to the Father before his death soon became the center of Chiara's life and that of her companions. John's chapter 17 was the magna carta for the adventure God drew them into. At the same time, they were very aware that unity—unity of many people in great diversity, in the image of the Holy Trinity—is not a project that

can be implemented by human strength alone.
Unity is a gift that comes from on high, a grace
to be invoked, as Jesus did. Gradually Chiara
realized that unity, in the fullest and deepest
sense of the word, springs forth from the hidden wound that God allowed her to discover.
Jesus Forsaken is the source of unity and is also
the supreme model for all those who want to
be an instrument of unity. It is thanks to him,
and with a life rooted in him, that unity is not
a utopia. Unity can be generated, with and by
virtue of him, by bravely embracing every affliction.

A gradual discovery

From a talk on "Jesus Forsaken and Life" [31]

Jesus Forsaken made himself known to us first
focolarine in a very gradual way.

In fact, at the beginning, he showed himself to
us as Love, and his light was such that we saw only
him, only him and the immensity of the love of
God that he was pouring out on the world.

He helped us overcome every suffering and he
filled us with pure joy. He cancelled out all our
sins. We saw him in the features of every brother
and every sister.

It was only later that he showed us himself as
the way to unity, as the secret and key to building
unity. Our exclusive love for him was the indispensable condition for us to be consumed in one,

in order to generate to unity an infinite number of persons, and thus to contribute to the fulfilment of "that they may all be one."

To form into one solid block your community

From a letter perhaps to Sr. Josefina and Sr. Fidente[32]

January 5, 1947[33]

In carrying out God's will, which consists entirely in *loving God and our neighbor to the point of being consumed in unity,* you will find the cross on which to crucify yourselves!

Don't be afraid! Rather, be glad! Go towards your goal! Jesus needs souls who know how to love him like this, *who choose him*, not for the joy that comes from following him, not for paradise or the eternal reward he is preparing for us, not just to "feel good."

No, no, no. *Only* because the soul, *thirsting for true love,* wants to be *consumed in one with him*—with that divine soul, sorrowful and passionate, tormented to the point of death, forced to cry out, "My God, my God, why have you forsaken me?"

Oh, my dear little sisters, we have *only one life, a short one at that.* Afterwards there will be paradise. We'll be with him forever. We'll follow the Lamb wherever he goes!

Don't be afraid of *suffering*, quite the contrary!

Either suffering or death!

But seek the suffering offered to you by the *Will of God*. Not only what is asked of you by your superiors in the simple commands of obedience, but the will of God which is *mutual love, the New Commandment, the Pearl of the Gospel!*

Do everything, *everything you can* to be *one* with each other and with all your sisters. They are your neighbors, so *love them as yourselves*.

Today is the Feast of the Holy Name of Jesus and *I am asking the eternal Father in Jesus' name for the grace that he may hasten the hour when all of you will be one, one heart, one will, only one thought.*

Which one? Jesus Crucified! Then, all attracted by the Cross, which attracts everyone to itself, you will work to *forge your small community into one solid block* and thus give the *Greatest Glory* to God!

Then God will live among you: you will feel it. You will enjoy his presence, he will grant you his light, he will inflame you with his love!

But to achieve this, you have to vow yourselves to *Jesus Crucified*.

He gave us the gift of unity

From a letter to Fr. Bonaventura da Malè, ofm cap.

March 13, 1948[34]

The cry of our soul is the cry of Jesus: "Unity or death!" This is our strength and the reality of each day.

I can honestly say, Brother, that if I hadn't had before my eyes that most painful cry of our beloved Jesus ("My God, my God, why have you forsaken me?"), I would have been overwhelmed, buried under the countless difficulties I encounter in consuming myself with souls. [...]

God abandoned by God! He was reduced to being a mere man because of his infinite love for humanity, to whom he had given God. Jesus was never only "man," but he did experience that infinite affliction by the Father in order to experience what "mortal sin" signifies.

Jesus! The Most Holy! The Most Pure! Love Itself!

He gave us Unity—the Ideal which is God himself.

For the others, unity, for ourselves, the abandonment

From a letter to Fr. Bonaventura da Malè, ofm cap.

"My God, my God, why have you forsaken me?"

March 30, 1948[35]

I'm convinced that unity, in its most spiritual, most intimate and most profound aspect, can only be understood by the soul for whom God has chosen, as his or her only portion in life, (…) Jesus Forsaken who cries out: "My God, my God, why have you forsaken me?"

Brother, now that I realize you understand this, which is the secret to unity, I would like to, and I could, speak to you about it for days on end. Know that Jesus Forsaken is everything. He is the guarantee of unity.

Every light on unity stems from that cry.

Choose him as the only aim, the only purpose, the only goal for your life and…generate an infinite number of souls to unity.

The book of Light that the Lord is writing in my soul has two sides: one, a page shining with mysterious love: *Unity*. The other page, shining with mysterious pain: Jesus Forsaken. They are two sides of the same coin. I show the page of unity to everyone. For me and for those who are with me on the front lines of unity, *our only portion is Jesus Forsaken.*

We've chosen to climb the mountain toward extreme abandonment.

Unity is for the others; for us, it's the abandonment. Which one? The one that Jesus (reduced nearly to a mere man in order to deify us) suffered: extreme pain, the sum total of all suffering, the pain as great as...God! "My God, my God, why have you forsaken me?" To search for him like the spouse in the Song of Songs is our supreme duty, as those who have been hurled onto the front lines by infinite love.

Search for him in our brothers and sisters who are sinners...without God! In them he is crying out: "My God, my God..." Search for him in all the external abandonments, but especially those that are deep and hidden...all the ones he sows along the path of life.

Run to where there is no unity and bring it

From a letter to Fr. Valeriano Valeriani, ofm conv., and to the other brothers in his community in Assisi

April 1, 1948[36]

Let's make the *unity between us* (which gives us the fullness of joy, peace, and *strength*) the springboard to run, to leap to wherever there is not unity, and *bring it there*!

In fact, just as Jesus preferred the Cross for himself, and not Mount Tabor, let's also prefer to be with those who are not *in unity*, so as to suffer with him and to ensure that our love is pure love! Then let us bring those people whom the Lord has given us, and have been won over, into the little sheepfold of Jesus: Unity.

It's for this reason, Brothers, that we crusaders of Unity have chosen as our only goal in life, as our everything: Jesus Crucified who cries out: "My God, my God, why have you forsaken me?"

This is Jesus in maximum pain! Infinite disunity so that he can give perfect unity to us, which we will be able to reach only relatively here below and then completely in Paradise.

This Jesus who is suffering so infinitely is in need of consolation from us.

And what is lacking to Jesus in such anguish?

What medicine would heal his pain?

God!

He's missing *God!*

How can we give God to him?

By staying united, we'll have him among us and Jesus who is born from our unity will console our Crucified Love!

This is why we should increase our unity in its quantity of love and of souls! We want the King to grow to gigantic proportions among us! And then we'll go out seeking to recompose every disunity, especially because in every disunited soul we hear the groan, more or less loudly, of our Jesus who is crying out.

Brothers, let us love Jesus, and especially let's be the angels of his abandonment!

I've experienced that every soul that finds itself on the front lines in Unity and for Unity can resist only by drawing on a Suffering-Love as strong as that of Jesus Crucified and Forsaken!

To make unity invincible

From a letter to Fr. Raffaele Massimei, ofm conv

Trent, April 23, 1948[37]

At times, the will of God is pain, abandonment and torture. To desire it as *the only "preference" of your soul* means rendering invincible the unity of our soul with God and therefore with our neighbor. [...]

Christ Crucified and Forsaken!

He's Everything!

If the world only knew him!

If the souls that follow Unity would only welcome him as their only goal, as their All! Then Unity would never again suffer imbalance, never again experience breakdowns.

Try, Father, to embrace him.

If I hadn't had him in the trials of life, there wouldn't be Unity, unless Jesus brought it about somewhere else.

Jesus Forsaken has won every battle within me, even the most terrible battles.

But it's necessary to be madly in love with him, who sums up every pain of the body and *of the soul*—the medicine, therefore, for every suffering of the soul.

Don't seek anything but him, yearn only for him; and when he draws near to your soul, rush out and embrace him, and find life in him!

Nothing is taken from us

From a letter to Fr. Raffaele Massimei, ofm conv.

Trent, June 15, 1948[38]

"...seek the things that are above..." [39]

God is invincible!

They give us Unity, we have God!

They take away Unity,[40] we have Christ on a cross who cries: "My God, my God, why have you forsaken me?"

And he is God! Even though he cries out, and precisely because he cries out, he is the very beautiful God of Love who gives the world a gift as big as God!

And he is our passion! Our deep and sincere passion.

The other day I was saying—perhaps to Father Leone—that Jesus Forsaken is truly "ours" because no one wants him—neither heaven nor earth! He is rejected by the earth and by heaven. Nothingness. *God.*

Oh! We've found it, Father, yes, we've found the precious pearl![41]

Oh! Our Love!

Oh! That fragment of a man, that "worm of the earth," that "mortal sin," that "crazy" person![42] He's all "ours!"

Oh! How our soul, which has discovered him, lets go of everything in order to embrace only him. Like the spouse in the Song of Songs, our soul sets out in search of our treasure! And we love him and *adore him*![43]

What lover wouldn't be drawn by such a Love?

Father, I'd like to run through the world, gathering hearts for him. And I feel that all the hearts in the world would never be enough for a love as great as God!

The light of unity in all its fullness

From a letter to Fr. Raffaele Massimei, ofm conv.

July 1948[44]

From this trial[45], it became clear that the one who was victorious was truly Jesus, in the height of his pain. If we had not kept the eyes of our soul fixed on him, we would not have known how to resist during that very cruel month and a half. And we would not have been able to sing the *Te Deum* even when the archbishop[46] seemed to withhold his approval.

Therefore, Jesus Forsaken is and will always be for us the *savior of unity*. Without him, everything would have collapsed. Even our Mother in heaven who had everything in hand, as our advocate, would not have been able to do as much.

It's Jesus in the height of his pain who gives impetus, strength, ardor, zeal, certainty and the solution to every problem of all the souls.

He completely stripped us of ourselves. He never abandons us, never, never, in all the most cruel misfortunes of life.

Whoever has understood this secret has the light of unity in all its fullness and the capacity to unite all the souls that the Lord gives to him or her.

To always love him more than life, more than joy, more than the Paradise of *Unity*! To always prefer him as the one and only treasure of the soul! To search for him in the present moment, to unite him to ourselves as the most beloved Spouse of our soul, never to leave him, never...this is what makes the soul strong.

Jesus Forsaken is the whole Gospel, all Love, all Light.

May the Lord help you, Father, to love him with a heart of flame.

He always has something new to tell us

From a letter

Trent, July 12, 1949[47]

Jesus Forsaken!

What's important is that when he passes by, we are attentive to hear what he wants to tell us, because he always has new things to say. Jesus Forsaken wants us to be perfect. He is the One and Only Teacher, and he uses circumstances to form us, to smooth out the rough edges of our character, to sanctify us. The only thing we have to do is to take all these voices of circumstances as his voice. All that happens around me happens *for me*; it is all a choral expression of God's love for me.

Chapter 2

The "Nothingness-Everything" of Love
Jesus Forsaken
in the experience of "Paradise '49"

In the period of light, or rather, of special illuminations, between the summers of 1949 and 1951, which Chiara later called "Paradise '49," the understanding of Jesus Forsaken, which until then had come especially from life, unfolded more profoundly. Love for him as a way of life became the starting point of a mystical experience that was not merely personal but also collective. Living mutual love with him as the model and allowing Jesus-Eucharist "to fuse them in unity,"[48] became for Chiara and her followers the path which led them into the heart of God, the Trinity, the bosom of the Father (cf. Jn 1:18). This experience opened wide a new vision of the world, of life and relationships, of the human person and of creation to the point of illuminating the ultimate destiny of all things, that is, paradise, and its negation, hell. At the heart of this understanding of God and the world is the paradox of Love, as revealed in the abandonment of Jesus on the cross. As God-man, he descended to the extreme depths of evil, and in him nothingness and everything met and coincided. From the notes that speak of the experience of those years, we have collected in this chapter a number of passages that can offer insights for meditation on Jesus Forsaken. The headings and introductions to the various excerpts offer some underlying perspectives, although a real deepening and complete overview cannot be presented here. Another point to bear in mind is the use of mystical language which, as in comparable experiences in the history of spirituality, expresses itself sometimes in strong and paradoxical terms.[49]

1. The Whole Gospel...Contained in That Cry[50]

As is known, the cornerstone of the story told in the four Gospels is Jesus' death on the cross and his resurrection. It is from this perspective that the first Christian community re-read the whole story of Jesus. With charismatic intuition, Chiara Lubich, after years of impassioned love for Jesus Forsaken, reached the same understanding. It seemed to her that the whole Gospel can be summarized in Jesus' gift of love to the point of the abandonment and in his resurrection. In him, we can find the synthesis not only of all the pain and evil present in the world and assumed by him, but also of every virtue, in the spirit of the beatitudes, which are the pivotal point of all the teaching of Jesus. This is the constant background of the experience of light that characterized the years 1949–1951.

The Word fully opened up

From a text on the experience of the summer of 1949

April 8, 1986[51]

Living one Word and then another and yet another, we came to realize that, putting any Word of God into practice, in the end the effects were the same. For example, living the Word: "Blessed are the pure in heart..." or "Blessed are the poor in spirit..." or "Blessed are the meek..." or "Love your neighbor as yourself" or "Do not do to others what you would not have done to you" brought us to the same conclusion, obtained for us the same effects.

The fact is that every Word, even though expressed in human terms and in different ways, is Word of God. But since God is Love, every Word is charity. We believed that we had discovered charity beneath every Word.

And when one of these Words came down into our soul, it seemed to us that it was transformed into fire, into flame; it was transformed into love. It could be said that our inner life was all love. [...]

So far as I recall, the last Word we had been living in that period was, "My God, my God why have you forsaken me?" And Jesus Forsaken appeared to us as the Word par excellence, the Word totally unfolded, the Word completely opened out. All that was needed, therefore, was to live him.

In that way, everything was made simple. Living him meant living the nothing of ourselves in order to be all for God (in his will) and for the others. [...]

Later we seemed to understand that in the Word in a certain sense is present Jesus, dead and risen. He is present dead in the negative part of the Word and risen in the positive[52].

Synthesis of all sufferings and of all virtues

From another text on the experience of the summer of 1949

June 30, 1961[53]

I don't remember exactly how it came to pass, but at that time, what gradually became ingrained in me in a very strong way was the conviction and the practice that followed on it, that Jesus Forsaken summed up the whole of the Gospel. And that, by loving him, all the virtues would blossom.

He seemed to us to be in synthesis the ascetic practice God was proposing to us, and that, by living him, we would be able to live Christ in us.

In Jesus Forsaken, there were all sufferings, all loves, all virtues, all sins (having made himself "sin") and in him we all found ourselves in every instant of our lives.

He, so close to death, was in synthesis every physical suffering and every moral and spiritual suffering.

He was every love in synthesis: he was "father" for having regenerated us; he was "mother" in the labor pains of our divine birth; he was brother, friend.

He was the synthesis of the virtues: the *pure* one, to the point of being detached from every divine consolation, he who was God; the *poor* one, poor of everything...even of the sense of his divinity. He was the obedient one, because he was losing everything in the Father, his Authority.

In fact, in that cry he appeared to us to be suffering and love together.

He was made "sin" for us sinners, rebellion, division, excommunication, and so forth, out of love. I do not know how to link these two terms: love and pain that in Jesus Forsaken appeared to us to be one single thing, so that one could not exist without the other.

By living Jesus Forsaken, we had come to understand how he had made himself *nothing* and in this *nothing* was our life. Being like him, out of love for him, the nothing that we really are. We nothing, he everything.

Jesus Forsaken is everything—call him by name

September 6, 1949[54]

It is beautiful to live Jesus Forsaken in the present moment and to call him by name. I have observed that Jesus Forsaken is all:

he is all pains,

he is all loves,

he is all virtues,

he is all sins,

(if he made himself "sin,"[55] he made himself—out of love—all sins,)

he is all realities.

For example: Jesus Forsaken is the mute, the deaf, the blind, the starving, the tired, the desperate, the betrayed, the failure, the fearful, the thirsty, the timid, the mad, and all the vices! The darkness, sadness...

He is boldness[56], he is Faith, Love, Life, Light, Peace, Joy, Unity, Wisdom, the Holy Spirit[57], the Mother, the Father, the Brother, the Spouse, the All, the Nothing, affection, effectiveness, bedazzlement, sleep, wakefulness etc. He is all the most opposite things: beginning and end; infinitely great and small...And one can observe that he is never the same.

2. He Made Himself Sin...To Make Everything God

For the apostle Paul the good news, the heart of the Gospel, is that "Christ ransomed us from the curse of the law, by becoming a curse for us" (Gal 3:13). "For our sake he made him to be sin who did not know sin, so that we might become the righteousness of God in him" (2 Cor 5:21). There is now no reality that is not reached and inhabited by Jesus, no space that is left "outside of God." The Letter to the Colossians affirms: "For in him all the fullness of God was pleased to dwell, and through him God was pleased to reconcile to himself all things, whether on earth or in heaven, by making peace through the blood of his cross" (Col 1:19–20; cf. Eph 1:10). It is against this background that the following passages will speak to us.

The fire that consumed all things in himself

July 20, 1949[58]

Jesus Forsaken is vanity and the Word; he is that which passes away and that which remains because he is God-Man, and as man he is the whole of creation, which is vanity of vanities, and as God he is the fire that consumes in itself all things, the nothing, divinizing it. Jesus Forsaken breathed into himself all the vanities and the vanities became him and he is God.

No longer is there emptiness upon earth, nor in Heaven[59]; there is *God*.

[...] Truly Jesus Forsaken made himself ugly to beautify all things, sin to take sin from the earth[60] and make all things: God; suffering to take what is ill from the world and reduce pain to love.

Look at one another as God sees us

July 20, 1949[61]

Jesus is Jesus Forsaken.

Jesus Forsaken is Jesus.

In every soul I find *Jesus*. If it is in perfect union with God, it is the whole Jesus.

If it is not, it will be 30% Jesus and 70% Jesus Forsaken or... in other proportions.

If it is in mortal sin, it is 100% Jesus Forsaken and Heaven rejoices when one of these souls returns because in the darkness of that soul another heaven is born. The 99 heavens of the righteous were there already.

July 24, 1949[62]

Those who are in the Father, having come through a long course of sinning, by God's pure mercy, are *equal* before God to the innocent who are there on the strength of *loving*.

Indeed, in that moment when, recognizing themselves as sinners, they rejoiced (loving God more than their soul and this is pure love) in being like him made sin[63], they filled the entire void made by sin.

In this way they have arrived in Paradise by God's pure mercy (so having had everything for free) but at the same time by God's pure love spoken freely from his heart. There Above, indeed, Mercy and Love are *One*.

In Paradise we will not see where Christ in us comes from, whether by Mercy or by Love, but we will see that every soul is *all Mercy and all Love*: it is Jesus. In fact, Mercy is Jesus Forsaken. Love is Jesus. But Jesus Forsaken is Jesus.

So look at human beings as God will see them, not as you see them. Because he sees what is true!

The labor of a Divine Birth

The theology of the Church Fathers considers Christ Crucified as the new Adam from whose pierced side the Church was born as the new Eve, recognizing in the blood and water that flowed from Christ's side, the origin of the Baptism and Eucharist that make us children of God. The fourth Gospel has its own way of indicating this reality: "Then he bowed his head and gave us his spirit" (Jn 19:30), in Greek: parédōken tò pneūma, which can also mean "the gift," "the handing over of the Spirit," which united Jesus to the Father. Chiara Lubich turns her attention to Jesus' cry of abandonment on the cross with an insight that penetrates into the depths of the mystery. At that moment, the bond between him and the Father seemed to break, to the point that he no longer resembled God, but only man. Thus the Spirit, who binds the Father and the Son, was communicated to us, opening the way for us to become children of God: the Church was born.

July 25, 1949[64]

Jesus Forsaken is maternal love. His cry represents the pangs of a Divine Birthing of human beings as children of God.[65]

In that moment the Church was started, because in that moment there came forth from him the children of God.

In fact, in that moment he gave the Holy Spirit who was to come down—after the Ascension—upon the Apostles gathered together with our Heavenly Mother.

Jesus was never more God[66]

In the abandonment, Jesus seemed to lose his bond with the Father, and yet he was more than ever identified with the Father, becoming the father of the new creation, the origin of the Church, which is his Body.

Tonadico, Italy, July 10, 1950[67]

Being *human* [Jesus] felt his forsakenness as pain, and yet he was never more God. The Father saw him equal to himself: Father, and he distinguished him from himself.

Jesus in his forsakenness is so much Jesus that he becomes Father and then the Father forsakes him in order to reunite him to himself in an even higher way.

Jesus never loved the Father as much as when he felt forsaken.

3. The Pupil of God's Eye

Jesus' abandonment is not only the deepest possible suffering and a human tragedy, but it also reveals the dynamism of love brought to its height, the measure and fullness of Love as it is in God. That wound, an everlasting emptiness, is like the "pupil of the Eye of God," a "window" through which we can contemplate, as far as it is possible, the mystery of unity and distinction of the three divine Persons. But it is also a "window" through which God looks at us with an infinite Love that transforms everything. The result is a new vision of all things, an ontology of love, the key to which lies in Jesus' abandonment, death and resurrection. The mystery of non-being/being is a key for the interpretation of human life and the entire universe.

Through the wound of the abandonment

August 1949[68]

Jesus is Jesus Forsaken. Because Jesus is the Savior, the Redeemer, and he redeems when he pours the Divine upon humanity through the Wound of his Forsakenness that is the pupil of the Eye of God upon the world: an infinite Void through which God looks upon us, the window of God thrown open upon the world, and the window of humanity through which we see God.[69] The Eye of God on the world is the Heart of Christ, but its pupil is that Wound.

Seeing from the point of view of the "One"

November 6, 1949[70]

[...] the vision is from Above, from the One, from the Peak, from God, who alone can judge things exactly, because he alone sees them in their true place, in proportion to all the rest. And like him, the soul sees too, since it is placed in him through the wound of Jesus Forsaken, which is to say that it has made *Jesus Forsaken* the only Ideal of its life, so as to have Unity, which is God, wholly in itself and to be in him.

Love is and is not at the same time

The event of Jesus' abandonment on the cross reveals the dynamics of love as non-being/being, that is, how to become nothingness, out of love for the other, and being fulfilled precisely by this. The result is an original anthropological vision, purely evangelical, personified by Mary in her total openness and availability to God and to others.

July 26, 1949[71]

Jesus Forsaken, because he is not, is.[72]

We are, if we are not. If we are, we are not.

We must be "without a thought" because we are children of God. The children of God do not have thoughts. Only when we do not have thoughts will our mind be totally open and constantly receive God's Light and be a channel.

Likewise, we must be without will so as to be capable of God's will.

And without memory so as to remember only the present moment and live "ecstatically" (outside ourselves).

Without flights of imagination so as to see Paradise also with the imagination,[73] because Paradise is the Dream of dreams.

There are emptinesses of different dimensions, just as there are fullnesses of different dimensions.

Our Heavenly Mother was infinitely[74] empty, and so invincible. Who could ever find her to strike her if she were not there?

The awareness of our nothingness ought to be infinite so that God may dwell in us. We must have the nothingness of Jesus Forsaken, which is infinite nothingness[75]. So then the Holy Spirit will repose in us.[76]

4. This is How to Become God: Love

The passages that follow combine in an "existential" dimension the anthropological vision that derives from Jesus Forsaken—the Man par excellence—that is, from the event of his abandonment, death and resurrection. The more we enter into this way of being, the more we will live our lives "in a divine way," as children of God, as new creatures, where the human is imbued with Love, with the Spirit of God.

Love must be distilled

September 2, 1949[77]

Love is to be distilled all the way to being only Holy Spirit.[78] It is distilled by passing it through Jesus Forsaken. Jesus Forsaken is the nothing, is the point, and through the point (= Love reduced to the extreme, having given everything) passes only Simplicity that is God: Love. Only Love penetrates...

Jesus Forsaken, embraced, locked to one's self, wanted exclusively as our only all, he consumed in *one* with us, we consumed in *one* with him, made Pain with him Pain: here lies everything. Here is how we become *God, Love*.[79]

Rome, Italy, November 23, 1950[80]

Being God's will made actual in the present moment is loving God with all your heart, your mind....[81] It is being God. It is living Jesus Forsaken and, that is, emptiness of self in order to be God.

5. Losing God in Oneself for God in Our Brothers and Sisters

Jesus' love to the point of experiencing being forsaken by the Father has filled every void that we or others may leave on this earth. This gift, received in faith, paves the way to union with God and, if reciprocated with our love for the Forsaken One, leads us to share in the very life of God. Jesus' love in his forsakenness becomes the key to build relationships with everyone, without exception. It becomes the way to bring others together in unity. Here we see the foundation of a spirituality, which is not merely individual, but also ecclesial, a "mysticism" of living together and of fraternity, called for by John Paul II, Benedict XVI and Pope Francis as a prerequisite to implement the Church-as-communion and to achieve its mission of unity within humanity.[82]

With everyone be in a position to learn

August 28, 1949[83]

To take into self the All it is necessary to be the nothing as Jesus Forsaken.

And on the nothing everyone can write...It is necessary to put ourselves before everyone in a position from which to learn, for we have something to learn in reality. And only the nothing gathers all into itself and clasps to itself each thing in unity; it is necessary to be *nothing* (Jesus Forsaken) before each brother or sister[84] in order to clasp *Jesus* to ourselves in them: "Whatever you did..."[85] And what will be the final examination of the soul that for the whole of its life has clasped Jesus to itself? That has made itself *ONE* with him? It will pass from examinee to examiner.[86]

To give all of ourselves

September 6, 1949[87]

Father, Jesus, Mary, us.

The Father forsook Jesus and Mary *for us.*

Jesus accepted being forsaken by the Father and forsook His Mother *for us.*

Mary accepted being forsaken by the Father (sharing the forsakenness of the Son) and by the Son *for us.*

We therefore are placed in the foreground. It is love that does these crazy things.

Thus *for our brother or sister* we must leave Father and Son and Mother: our brother or sister is our Heaven here below.[88]

To enter into the other person

Trent, Italy, September 8, 1949[89]

Now we can enter into the other in various ways: pushing ourselves in like someone big who wants to get in through a small door...and this is how someone acts who does not listen to the very end (someone who does not die *totally* in the brother or sister who is Paradise for me, the Kingdom for me) and wants to give replies gathered bit by bit in his or her own head that may be inspired but are not that breath of the Holy Spirit which will give life to the other.

There are those (passionate lovers of Jesus Forsaken) who more willingly die than live and who listen to their brother or sister all the way to the end, not worried about the reply, which will be given in the end by the Holy Spirit who summarizes in few words, or in one, all the medicine for that soul.

Move into God in my neighbor

November 6, 1949[90]

And so, when throughout the day the soul has willingly lost God in itself in order to be transferred into God in its brother or sister (for each is equal to the other, just as two flowers in that garden are the work of an identical maker), and has done so out of love for Jesus Forsaken who leaves God for God (and precisely God in self for the God present or being born in the brother or sister...), when it returns to itself or better to the God within (because alone in prayer or in meditation), it will find again the caress of the Spirit who—because he is Love—*is Love* in truth, since God cannot fall short of his word and gives to the one who has given: he gives love to the one who has loved.

Thus darkness and unhappiness disappear with aridity and all the bitter things, leaving behind only the full joy promised to the one who has lived Unity [...]

But it is necessary to lose the God in self for God in our brothers and sisters. And this is done only by the one who knows and loves Jesus Forsaken.

6. Being a Sacrament of Love in the World

The Church, as Vatican II affirms, is "in Christ like a sacrament or as a sign and instrument both of a very closely-knit union with God and of the unity of the whole human race." (Lumen Gentium, 1). The following passages express the participation in the mission of Christ that involves all the people of God and also individual believers, who are called to become increasingly more, as the Church Fathers said, "Church-souls." The affirmations made by Chiara in the following pages ought to be understood in this context: an "I" identified with the "ecclesial we,"—and ultimately with the "I" of Jesus Forsaken and Risen.

Give me all who are lonely

Trent, Italy, September 1, 1949[91]

Lord, give me all who are lonely...I have felt in my heart the passion that fills your heart for all the forsakenness in which the whole world is drifting.

I love every being that is sick and alone. Even the suffering plants cause me pain...even the animals that are alone.

Who consoles their weeping?

Who mourns their slow death?

Who clasps to their own heart, the heart in despair?

My God, let me be in this world the tangible sacrament of your Love, of your being Love; let me be your arms that clasp to themselves and consume in love all the loneliness of the world.

I am humanity

September 6, 1949[92]

I feel I live in me all the creatures of the world, all the Communion of Saints. Really: because my *I* is *humanity, with all the people that were, are, and will be.* I feel and I live this reality: because I feel in my soul both the delight of Heaven and the anguish of humanity that is all *a great Jesus Forsaken.* And I want to live him totally, this Jesus Forsaken. I live him adding the drop of my pain of the moment (which is my life, me made *Pain* as he is) *to his*. But already living him I live all Pain. Indeed, I live delighting in the nothingness I am in contrast to God.

For every mistake of my neighbor

August 1949[93]

For every mistake made by my brother or sister I ask forgiveness of the Father *as if* it were my own because my love takes possession of it. *Like this* I am Jesus. And I am Jesus Forsaken, always before the Father as Sin, and in the greatest act of love for my brothers and sisters and so for the Father.

Therefore, each sin is mine.

Like this, I am Jesus, Lamb of God who takes away the sins of the world. In fact, my love pays for them, burning them up.

"Jesus, hide yourself..."

The next two passages conclude the notes of 1949–1951 collected by Chiara under the title "Paradise '49."

September 1951[94]

Jesus, hide yourself, for I see you everywhere.

Even when I sweep and dust my room, I see you, for with your cry, you swept away sin from the world and you dusted minds of the hindrances that clouded your peace...

And if I wash my hands, I see you. You in that cry washed away sin from our souls.

You are All because you are Life in that moment of infinite death.

Work too, any work, I have seen and reduced to you, for work consumes energy and in this death there is you; and it produces something good and in this life, there is you.

An excess of love

September 22, 1951[95]

Cold freezes. But if it is excessive, it burns and cuts.

Wine strengthens. But if it is too much, it saps your strength.

Motion is as it is. But if it spins fast, it seems still.

The Spirit of God gives life, but it inebriates.

Jesus is Love because he is God. But his excessive love made him Jesus Forsaken who seems merely human.

Chapter 3

"The Root of the Tree"
With Jesus Forsaken
during the time of trial

Joy and pain go hand in hand, not only in every person's journey, but also in the birth and growth of a work of God. Even though from the very beginning Chiara was both convinced and skilled in the adventure of this life for unity, she had an experience in the 1950s that would forever remain paradigmatic. In addition to harrowing personal trials, as are often found in great spiritual figures, the authenticity of the charism of Chiara and the growing Focolare Movement was under study by the Holy See for over a decade, until its approval in March 1962. Those years were marked by pain, suspension and darkness, but the fruits were abundant. It is enough to think of the steady development of the "Mariapolis" (the summer meetings in the Dolomites), which reached its peak during the summer of 1959, with a total attendance of over 12,000 people. In her writings, Chiara compares this time to a long gestation period, during which the Church, even in the most painful moments, was always a mother. She said: "It was not yet the moment for us to be born as a distinct reality in the Church. Indeed, it appeared clear to us that we were passing through the period when our movement was still being formed, as a new child of the Church, in the Church's womb."[96] We will now enter into this experience through some short thoughts, published in one of Chiara's first meditation books.

Only those who pass through the ice of suffering[97]

The diameter of the foliage of a tree often corresponds to the diameter of its roots.

Our heart opens up to Christ's love according to how much we have suffered and offered for him.

We cannot be fathers and mothers of souls unless we are nailed to the cross.

At the climax of desolation, God often asks of us a silent suffering known to him alone. However, through suffering borne and overcome in this way, an abundance of life surges through the Mystical Body.

Only those who pass through the ice of suffering reach the furnace of love.

"Without the shedding of blood there is no forgiveness of sins." [98]

Likewise, without the shedding of tears, there are no conversions.

At times, God asks for our tears and we see the fruit they bear. At other times, unaware of the fruits, we offer our tears to him, and he scatters them like divine dew in the most parched and arid corners of the earth.

A car keeps on going according to how much gas is in the tank. A work of God grows according to how much suffering is transformed into love.

1. The storm

In the letters at the beginning of the movement, Chiara already revealed how aware she was that trials would always be part of the journey through life with God.

Jesus digs deep to lay the foundation

From a letter to Fr. Bonaventura da Malè, ofm cap.

Ortisei, Italy, September 8, 1948[99]

You shared with me the odyssey of your life. It's precisely the logical course that Jesus takes.

At first, he gives us the illusion, and the happiness, that *we* have found *him*. Then, so that nothing human can block the Work of God, he permits periods of darkness, disturbing, distressing moments, so that we can see *who we are*. Then, aware of our nothingness and of our wretchedness, we throw ourselves again into him, with total trust only in him.

Therefore, Father, see your life as being guided by the Divine Hand. Just when you perhaps felt most abandoned, Jesus was carving out the foundation, in order to then construct the house = himself.

God works on the souls who give themselves totally to him

From a letter to Fr. Bonaventura da Malè, ofm cap.

November 2, 1948[100]

It has been my experience that when souls give themselves to Love, without holding anything back, God takes them at their word and works on them, breaking them, crushing them, consuming them.

It will be the same for you; you will be like gold in a furnace. Now you can enjoy the "honeymoon" of the meeting of your soul with him.

Next will come the reciprocal giving of gifts.... until he possesses everything of you.

Then your mind will be totally imbued with light and your will be full of his fire which is Love.

May that day come!

However, it is not for us to contemplate the work God is doing in our own soul.

For our part, we should work for God in the Christian community, which means to look around and see the hearts near to us and love them *as ourself* to the point of being able to give them our very own Ideal, in the measure that God has given it to us.

Every person who is consumed in unity with us, however, will cost us our *life*.

We have to be perfectly dead to ourselves in order to be *one* with those who are next to us.

Pruning the growing tree

From a letter to Fr. Bonaventura da Malè, ofm cap. and to another three religious priests

February 17, 1949[101]

For a few months now, the new sun of Charity has risen on the horizon of your lives and melted you into one heart so that the Lord—already certain of your faithfulness—now puts your virtue to the test.

Yesterday, when I learned that the Divine Will, the fatherly Hand of God, had begun the necessary and beneficial work of pruning the growing plant, I could hardly believe it. I was expecting it, but not so soon! And Jesus immediately made me see what a special love he has for you. My little brothers, if anything has taken up residence in your hearts that doesn't resemble joy for what is happening, then that heart must admit that it hasn't understood *Unity*.

What is happening to you is the logical consequence of the Ideal that we've proposed for our lives.

Among you—who are united in his name—is Jesus. You form *Jesus*, and Jesus can only live as Jesus! [...]

This apparent detachment, this forced disunity from your brothers and sisters outside the college who struggle, live and suffer for the same Ideal as you, isn't this perhaps a little *Jesus Forsaken* for you? [...]

It's only by embracing Jesus Forsaken *with your whole heart*, who is all one wound in his body and all darkness in his soul, that you will be formed in *Unity*. [...]

Remain in his love—loving one another as he has loved each one of you—and then his and your Ideal will triumph. Your entire college will be a *focolare* [hearth], a living temple of the Holy Spirit, and you will be the *living* stones.

Draw light from him to pour out on the world

From a letter to Fr. Giovanni Festa, Oratorian

Ostia, Italy, March 31, 1950[102]

I have nothing anymore, Father.

I can assure you of that.

I don't have the Focolare centers, nor the movement, nor our Unity, nor what I had before giving myself to him.

I have only J.F. [Jesus Forsaken]. He never leaves me, that's for sure.

He is there where everything is lacking.

In obscurity, in solitude, in the cold, wherever no one wants to be.

And we with him, to draw from him the Light to be poured out in torrents onto the world.

Father, I have seen clearly that we will become saints only on the condition that we go right to the end in our Ideal.

2. The Hour of the Birth

Chiara, in her book, *The Cry*, referring to two talks given in December 1971, spoke of Jesus Crucified and Forsaken as the model of unity with the Church. By virtue of her charism, unity with those who represented the Church was crucial. "Only in the Church and through the Church were we united with God." [103] It is thus understandable how painful the investigation on the part of the Holy

See must have been, since its outcome seemed uncertain and could have also led to the dissolution of the movement. "For the Church it was something simple, it was a duty for them," Chiara writes, "but for us it meant suspension and uncertainty." [104] It was a journey in which she seemed to relive in some way the abandonment of Jesus by the Father, but then also his resurrection. It is a unique experience, which sheds a great light on ecclesial relations, especially in very difficult moments.[105] A few salient passages of the book, *The Cry*, follow, referring the reader to the volume itself for a more in-depth analysis.

We felt we had been formed to be "Church" [106]

In the Christian view, there is no cross without a resurrection, even though the resurrection may not come for years. "Cross" and "resurrection" are two aspects of a single reality. And only the resurrection explains the cross.

John calls the two together "glorification."

Consequently, one cannot understand the painful period of our history without taking into account some later periods, and, most of all, the present.

Christianity, when newly born, looked like a beautiful and healthy little plant, but it needed lengthy suffering and long persecutions that made it grow and spread. Only 300 years after its birth was it present all over the known world.

A few years after the birth of the Focolare, a new current of evangelical life and a new Christian community had come to life. They were beautiful in the eyes of God, but as the logic of the gospel requires, along came the death of that seed, the pruning of that little tree. [...]

Now, years later, we well understand that if we had to pass through trials, like all others who commit themselves to a life of radical faith (and, indeed, we felt a need of trials), they should not be unlike the ones that had tested our leader: Jesus Forsaken.

He had experienced forsakenness from the one he called Father, *Abba*, whom he loved so much.

To us, these trials in one way or another had to come through whoever represents the Father here on earth, or our Mother, that is, the Church, whom we loved so much, and in whom and for whom we wanted to spend our lives.

But just as Jesus ascended to the right hand of the Father after that trial in which he had uttered his cry and become almost another Father, after our trial was over, we felt we had been made "Church."

And we *were* Church. We *are* Church. [...]

In guiding the Church, God gave it the light not to leave us abandoned. He was the founder and the architect of the marvelous Work that was to be born; he had nourished it with his Spirit; it had been formed solely by him.

When he saw it beautiful, and complete in its essential parts, the time arrived for its birth—March 23, 1962—but not without the accompanying pain.

To not have and not be: this is the secret of growth[107]

The trial that touched us all, some to a greater degree, others less, really had the symptoms of a trial from God. If, on the one hand, it seemed we had to die, on the other hand, the will of God told us to live. While circumstances seemed to tell us everything was finished, sometimes even the very next day God would arrange for the Church herself to make it possible for us to carry on.

So ours truly was a pain similar to that of Jesus Forsaken, who at the same time *was* and *was not* forsaken. Like him we too felt abandoned, but the Work of God lived and grew. [...]

Nonetheless, while under the pressure of trials during that whole period, we still saw *rays of light.* Our work continued, even though seasoned with the bitterness of situations that at times took our breath away, of suspensions that sometimes discouraged us.

We were aware that we had to work, and work on the very basis of that void, faithful to him in moments when the shadow of the cross soured our joy in serving him.

Indeed, they were precious moments for us. Working in pain, we felt we were building the movement on rock. [...]

During that period of trial, our love for Jesus Forsaken was increasing: seeking him, preferring him, loving him without analyzing the pain, never taking our gaze off him, joyfully welcoming him, not merely putting up with him, but loving him, living together with him, loving him exclusively. [...]

Meanwhile, the Lord continued to work on us. With the scalpel of his love he brought us to detach ourselves from everything in order to have nothing but him. We were led to be detached from what we had and from what we were. This was the freedom of the children of God: not to have and not to be. Not to have what we believed to be ours, but knew was really God's. Not to be ourselves, in order to be him.

The outward fruits we witnessed were so many and so rich that we realized how necessary the cross is to the spreading of the Gospel.

Had the cross not been with us, we would not have had the equilibrium necessary to bring forward the Work of God. Suffering is useful to God as a means of removing the vigor of our pride and self-love, allowing him to operate in us undisturbed.

We exulted joyfully for the *fruits* but, having the cross, we did not exalt *ourselves*. [...]

And yet, one thought above all never left me. It was the effect of a very painful interior trial, which at that time burned within me more than ever: I understood who I was and who he was. He was everything. I was nothing. He was strength. I was weakness.

The very experience of my own weakness convinced me that the fruits we were bearing, those thousands of conversions, could not be the result of anything else but a Work of God.

3. Life Emerges From Death

The letters written by Chiara in the mid-1950s to her followers reflect the living experience of that period: an unquenchable passion for unity, the weight and darkness of moments when everything seems to collapse. But they also reflect the faithful and ever deeper love for Jesus Forsaken, who reveals himself as the secret to be able to face any external and internal trial, spiritual or physical, and the gratitude for always new fruits.

The Ideal that burst forth from that wound

From a letter to the men and women focolarini

1956[108]

Look, we focolarini have a very big cross. When we started living in a focolare house we resolved to choose Jesus Forsaken, and he has now appeared.

We know we are loved by God, perhaps we are even given special preference, and we know we are in the heart of the Church, but a shadow hangs over us, and you know it.

Jesus could not have permitted a suffering more suitable for us who follow Jesus Forsaken. . . .

But we know that life has to be paid for. The life which comes to many souls through us is produced by death. *We arrive at the fire only by passing through ice.*

As far as we know, this spirit of unity is something that no one else has. It is a gift we cannot measure! It is the result of the presence of Jesus, who has come to live among us...because he found 'poor little women,' 'poor fishermen.'

Let's hold on tight to our Jesus Forsaken and not let go of him for anything. [...]

Let's declare ourselves ready to follow him like this, or in any way he wishes, for the rest of our lives, and to continue loving him even after our death, through all those to whom we have managed to transmit this Ideal of ours, the genuine Ideal which...flows from that wound.[109]

Don't be afraid, little flock!

From a letter to the men and women focolarini at a time when it seemed that Chiara was being asked to leave the movement.

Grottaferrata, Italy, April 4, 1957[110]

And yet, believe me, in this horrifying scenario that is set before us so frequently, and that culminates in a certain type of pain, which you know about, there is something very majestic, something indescribably beautiful. *It is the clear certainty that this is a Work of God.*

It is the *Work of God* because it is not our work, not of anyone of us.

It is the *Work of God* because, once complete, even the instrument that God used can be removed.

It is the *Work of God* because whoever knows your heart, the heart of the majority of you, knows that no obstacle will ever stop you. No matter what happens, you will know how to see only the adorable Face of the Spouse of your souls. He is the *only* one you have followed along this way, and, embracing him under a new form, in a new aspect, *but truly embracing him*, he will find you purer, stronger, more ardent, more beautiful, more alone, more united. He will see you as his dearest children, formed by his love, illuminated by his light, radiating his light in the world.

Oh, don't be afraid little flock, because it has pleased God to give you the kingdom and his kingdom is wherever souls are united, having passed through the Wound of the abandonment.

I tell you the truth: I don't know what will become of me, as far as the affairs of this earth are concerned.

However, I know very clearly what will happen to all of you.

One day I asked Jesus with a heart of a mother to save you, and ever since then I have felt a sense of certainty. *I am certain that God will save you*, and with you, he will save his Work. It's in his interest, and you, many of you, will become saints.

This is the conclusion for those who love Jesus Forsaken without measure.

I will do his Will, whether I am close or far from you, putting my hand to the new plow that God will assign me, without looking back.

Our Lady, who has loved me so much, will help me not to waste time in memories or in going back to the past.

Notwithstanding how wretched I am, I am happy to have spent thirteen years in such direct service to a work that is hers.

She will take you all under her mantle as her specially chosen children, and she will take me, too, wherever the Will of God will desire, and we will all meet in her Immaculate Heart.

That's life...just a little more and then...Life itself!

All of you, as worthy children of Mary, accept from her hands everything that might happen, repeating her attitude, her standing firm at the foot of the cross in the *stabat Mater.*

Remember that *nothing is lacking to the one who embraces Jesus Forsaken and keeps Jesus in the midst.*

He in our midst will save each and every thing, every aspect of his Work, every word that is spoken to built it up.

Our drop in his chalice

From a letter to the men and women focolarini

This letter was written three days after the death of Pope Pius XII, who, just a week before, had explicitly blessed the Focolare Movement. The approval seemed to be near, and yet it didn't come until 1962.

Rome, October 12, 1958[111]

The Lord is certainly jealous of us. He wants us alone, with him, with him alone.

That maternal caress from the Church was so beautiful...but our Ideal does not spread through joys; they are not the way to buy souls. Souls are paid for with pain and, for us, with Jesus Forsaken.

I shared with the focolarine that, a few days ago, I told Jesus: "Who knows how you are with souls who love you! What attention, what love you must give them! If, on this earth, sincere human love is so noble, so admirable . . . who knows what God's love is like!"

And an answer rose spontaneously in my soul: "Yes, but the God who chose you, who chose all of you, is called *'Forsaken.'*" This name carved itself into my heart in a new way, more majestic and more solemn than before. It seemed to become my *surname.* [...]

How many times the word "Why?" comes to my lips!

But then I understand. "Yes," I tell him, "yes, yes, Jesus, take this gift, unite it with your own, convert souls and complete your Work. It is of no importance to us to know what will become of us; we know we are in the Church. We have always believed the Church is our 'mother,' and we have come to know her in that way, just like that. [...]

"And if it is worth something to put our drop of blood into your chalice, let this pain be for the Church, your Church, for the new Pope; in him we will see no one but you, love no one but you."

4. The Constant Training of the Cross

We conclude this chapter with three prayers that reflect, from different perspectives, the inner landscape of Chiara's soul in the long journey towards the recognition of the movement by the Church. Her relationship with Jesus in the trial of the abandonment supported her in that time, from beginning to end.

This is how I found you

(1957)[112]

When one speaks of love, Lord, people often think of it as something that is always the same.

But how many kinds of love there are!

I remember that when I met you, I wasn't worried about how to love you.

Perhaps because it was you who had met me, and you wanted to fill my heart.

I remember that sometimes I was all on fire, even though I felt the burden of my humanity as though I were carrying a heavy weight.

But already at that time, your grace enabled me to understand a little who I was and who you were, and I saw that flame as your gift.

Then you showed me where to find you.

"Under the cross," you told me, "under every cross is where I am. Embrace it and you will find me."

You told me many times and I do not remember all the arguments you used. But you finally convinced me.

Then, with each suffering I thought of you, and with my will I responded with my yes....

But the cross remained; my soul was bathed in darkness, I suffered torments of all kinds—how many crosses there are in life!

Then, later, you taught me to love you in my neighbor and so, when suffering came, I did not stop there but accepted it and, forgetting myself, turned my thoughts to the person next to me. After a few moments, when I would go back inside myself, I would find that my sorrow had vanished.

So it was for years and years: the constant training of the cross, the asceticism of love. I underwent many trials and you know all about them, because you have counted the hairs on my head and numbered them in your heart.

Now love is something else; it is not just an act of the will.

As soon as the dart of love hits, it lights up a flash of light in my soul and I find myself immersed in your love.

I have the impression that a film is being played in my spirit and it is the film of my daily life. However, Someone has turned up the speed so much that the individual scenes are no longer visible. The film is regulated in such a way that the frames that disappear are all the painful moments. Instead, what comes into evidence are the very sweet, prolonged, solemn and simple meetings with Love.

I knew that God is Love, but I had no idea it was anything like this.

Tired under the cross

Brussels, Belgium, Holy Week 1962[113]

Lament
We are tired, Lord,
 so tired under the cross
 and every little cross that appears
 makes the larger ones seem impossible to carry.
We are tired, Lord,
 so tired under the cross,

our tears tighten our throats,
we drink bitter tears.
We are tired, Lord,
so tired under the cross.
Hasten our time
for there is no more joy for us here,
nothing but desolation.
The good we love
is entirely up there,
while down here
we are tired, oh so tired,
under the cross.
The Virgin is beside us,
Beautiful, yet sad.
May she, in her solitude,
help ours in this hour.

Life

July 20, 1961[114]

Joys and sorrows,
hopes,
dreams fulfilled.
Maturity in life and thought.
Solidity.
A sense of duty
and a call of love from on High,
answered by
the integrity of our life.
Weariness.

Fire and conquest.
Storms.
Trust in God:
God alone.
Up.
Down.
Torrential rain,
 deep roots.
Fruits, fruits, fruits...
Darkening of the soul:
"My God, my God ..."
Then, sweet music from heaven,
 distant.
Then closer.
The drum roll:
victory!
Long is life,
 different the paths,
 near is the goal.
All,
everything,
always,
has,
has had,
one single destiny:
union with you.

Chapter 4

"The God of Today"
Dialogue and dedication to
make of humanity one family

"This is our Ideal: Jesus Crucified and Forsaken, in us and outside of us, in the whole world
that is waiting to be consoled and comforted,"
wrote Chiara in the 60s.[115] With the compass
of life aimed at him, an endless horizon opened
wide in front of her. Just as the poor were in
the foreground from the beginning, at the time
of discoveries and developments, so they were
always central, with all those in need. However,
very soon other scenarios emerged, such as
moral evil in its various facets, people with no
religious faith, the Church reduced to silence
and persecuted in Eastern Europe, the divisions
within Christianity. With prophetic clarity and
realism, Chiara faced up to the postmodern,
pluralistic, multicultural and multireligious
world, torn apart by the proliferation of numerous conflicts. In all these situations, the love
for Jesus Forsaken ensures that one does not
flee but rather addresses every challenge, with
concrete attention to individual persons, and

with actions, projects, social movements and initiatives for dialogue. Whoever has discovered Jesus Forsaken and sees his countenance in every pain and disunity, in every misfortune and division, cannot withdraw into a life of devotional piety or even comfortable intimacy, but rather will always be—with him—at the forefront, in the fracture, in contact with the "wounds," in order to find a solution. It is in this sense that Chiara saw Jesus Forsaken as "the God of our times," "the God of today." [116]

1. With Those Who Suffer

"Love Jesus Crucified in yourself, in the infinite variety of your sufferings, but love him most of all outside of yourself, in your brothers and sisters, in all your brothers and sisters. If you could have any preferences among them, love him in the greatest sinners, in the most wretched, the most ragged, the most repugnant, the most forsaken, the rejects of society, in all those most tortured by life." This is the course of action indicated by Chiara in one of the first books of her meditations. [117] This proposal, depending on the person and the situation, has been expressed in different ways, even in large scale projects, as for example, the Economy of Communion.

Start with those most in need

From an international conference call

June 27, 1991[118]

Our charism, at the beginning of the movement, made us focus our attention—even though we still lived at home with our families—on those around us who were the "least," such as the poor, the sick, the wounded, the prisoners, the homeless, the elderly, the children...

Later on, in the first focolare house in Piazza Cappuccini, we sought out those who were the least within our community [of people living this Ideal].

We tried to solve the problems of the first group by doing acts of love for them, which were seeds of the larger social projects and many works of mercy that would develop in the future. For the second group, we started a communion of goods among all of us.

Sharing, conversion, unity

From a talk on Jesus Forsaken[119]

Because of our love for Jesus Forsaken, light and peace shone out, not only in our souls, but in all those who were alone, disorientated, orphans, disheartened, failures, humiliated, without support in absurb situations—once they recognized him under those aspects. We chose him together. These people were the favorites among the members of the movement and we tried to share all the pain of their hearts. Then at the opportune moment, we would talk to them about Jesus, about his infinite love, especially for those who are mentioned in the beatitudes, and about the privilege they had to be able to share the cross with him, for their own good and the good of humanity.

We also explained to them the need to offer him our personal sufferings, in which we see nothing other than his face. [...]

Jesus came down on earth, becoming a human being, but on the cross, he annihilated himself, and in the abandonment, he seemed to be totally obliterated.

As a divine inclined plane, he has given *each and every person* on earth a chance to reach the Divine Majesty, in *whatever* moral or spiritual condition they find themselves, as long as they turn to him, transforming all the sufferings that oppress them into a coin of love as they follow him.

In this way, many people, little by little, also through our movement, have understood or experienced the words of Jesus, "Those who are well have no need of a physician, but those who are sick." (Mt 9:12)

[...]

Then there were the sinners and those far from the Church...and yet they are all members of the Mystical Body, or at least directed towards it.

In these brothers and sisters, too, we saw his face.

It was this love for Jesus Forsaken in them, besides the witness of the unity among us, that brought about, with the grace of God, the most varied conversions.

Social works and projects

From a talk given to a convention entitled, "Men and women religious and the challenges of society"

Castel Gandolfo, Italy, April 19, 1995[120]

Jesus Crucified and Forsaken: the key to unity, but also the mirror reflecting all the suffering in the world. [...]

Could there be anyone, no matter what his or her spiritual or physical pain, unable to identify with him?

That infinite torment became for us the panorama of every suffering in the world.

This is the way we have always thought and always tried to act accordingly. [...]

When the movement begins with the poor, with the needy, then we know that its life is starting in its own characteristic setting, and this promises development, fruits and vocations. [...]

Over the years, the great tree of the movement, whose nature is love, supernatural love, has grown and blossomed into many branches all over the world, with an abundance of flowers and fruits. These fruits include a variety of short-term or ongoing social or charitable projects. [...]

They are initiatives of different scope and size, but they all pulsate with life, because those who work in them have at heart Jesus Crucified and Forsaken who repeats to them: "You did it to me." [121] [...]

Our activities, and particularly those of the youth, are not limited to these. Every day they initiate activities for the benefit of those they call "the Jesus Forsaken of the moment." They help many people who are suffering due to natural disasters like earthquakes, fires, floods...or those tragedies provoked by people, like war. These young people have no peace until they give their own personal contribution, until they can hasten to those areas where death and suffering are commonplace. They invent all kinds of projects, according to the needs they see around them, collecting money, goods and even truckloads of useful things to be distributed.

Why do they do this?

Because of what Jesus said: "You did it to me."

To die for one's people

The Gen (young people living the Ideal of unity) have always attempted to involve their peers in the adventure of making the Gospel the code of their lives and working tirelessly for a better world. In 1977, Chiara launched an invitation to them to take a further step.

Message to the youth, published as an editorial in the "Gen" magazine

Rocca di Papa, Italy, November 3, 1977[122]
The goal, the purpose, the reason for which Jesus came on earth is contained in a phrase that is our program and the motto of the Gen and of all young people acquainted with the Gen spirit. Jesus came in order to *"die for his people."*

And note this, Gen, Jesus did not "die for his people" (who were, first of all, the Jewish people and then all of humanity) only on the cross. No! Jesus was *always* ready "to die for his people."

His life is the clearest example of this. [...]

He did it by approaching and healing the lame, the blind and the paralytics, people rejected by that society, which viewed suffering as a consequence of sin.

He did it by associating with sinners, prostitutes and thieves; by feeding the hungry, even to the point of working miracles for them, as he did with the multiplication of the loaves and fishes.

He did it by liberating those possessed by the devil; by raising people from the dead with his divine power, as he did with Lazarus and the daughter of Jairus.

Above all, he gave a message that was the motivating force behind all of these and the other magnificent and unique actions which he alone could do. [...]

This is how a person dies for their own people. The poor, the blind, the dead, the sinners of our days are perhaps called by different names. They are the drug addicts, the marginalized, the disabled, people with a partial vision of life (a vision that only considers this world, for example), people who hate, people who support crimes against human life at all stages and those who live in the most absurd immorality. We have lonely children of divorced parents suffering the consequences of not having a family; people who are sick and dying because of a lack of resources; the elderly who are abandoned; youth high on drugs; prisoners, and so on.

Today, Jesus would come "to die for *these* people," to save them from all these evils.

But Jesus came twenty centuries ago.

Today, he wants to return through us.

Jesus was young. He wants to return especially through young people! [...]

"Die for your own people," and draw all the young people you know to do the same—right now, every day.

Do this unceasingly in all your neighborhoods, in your schools, along the streets, everywhere.

2. "To Become a World-Person"

In the 1970s, Chiara had an intuition that in the future there would be great technological developments, globalization and a multicultural and multireligious society. This would cause, she foresaw, the crumbling of centuries-old cultural paradigms, which seemed to offer security and boundaries, but in reality were closed to outsiders and applicable only in certain contexts. She proposed a new humanism, and not just something theoretical, but also practical and concrete. How would this be possible? How can humanity live as one family, without eliminating diversity or causing cultural conflicts, but rather treasuring differences as a gift? In response to the youth of the Gen Movement, Chiara pointed to Jesus Crucified and Forsaken, who, at the very moment when his human life was collapsing, gave rise to a new world. Her talk to them seems equally relevant today, if not more so, and can be a light for anyone trying to live as a Christian in today's world. We offer here a summary, recommending the reading of the original text.

To the International *Gen Congress*

July 22, 1972[123]

That they may all be one

In the age of the atomic bomb, of the splitting of the atom, which people believed to be indivisible, heaven permitted that we discover a divine atomic bomb, which is the most powerful weapon of all: love. Instead of destroying the world, instead of leveling humanity to the ground, it raises it up to the greatest heights possible and bestows on it the highest dignity. It is the dignity of being a single people, the people of God, rather than people of many nations who live right next to one another, but who often fight and threaten each other like rude and dangerously overgrown children. It is a weapon that brings unity here on earth, not merely a human unity, but a divine one. It's the unity for which Christ prayed when, preparing to die for all of us, he said, "Father, that they may all be one." [...]

Jesus Forsaken: the divine atomic bomb

[...] If Constantine believed he saw a cross in the sky and understood from it, "In *this* sign you will be victorious," the Gen know that they will be victorious by using one means alone. This means is called "Jesus Forsaken," that is, Jesus in agony on the cross who cried out, "My God, my God, why have you forsaken me?"

It's precisely Jesus Forsaken who is the divine atomic bomb [...].

He is God who cries out "My God, my God..." In that cry, hurled by the God-man towards heaven, towards God, it seems—but it's not true—that the unity of God is broken. In reality, it's precisely in that suffering and through that suffering of Jesus that we can find the solution, every solution, to recompose in unity and harmony all the disunities that we and everyone else experience—individuals and whole nations alike! Through Jesus Forsaken, the unity of the world can be accomplished.

But before trying to explain how this remedy can be applied to the world of today, which is calling for unity, communion and peace everywhere, I would like to take a look with you at the current situation of the world.

The need for a worldwide communion

[...]

I want to speak about the new situation we find ourselves in, because of the irreversible encounter of peoples and civilizations in every part of the world. This encounter was made possible and encouraged by the explosive development of the communications media and by the colossal progress in the field of technology. All of this has certainly brought about a great deal of good, because there is a greater circulation of news, knowledge, facts, events, traditions and mentalities, causing everything to be put in common, and impelling everyone to move beyond their own cultural and national mentality, which up until now had regulated their lifestyle. [...]

There is another side to the coin, however.

People today are not always prepared for this kind of encounter with those who are different from them[...].

The limitations of our culture

[...]

Concepts, traditions and mentalities that seemed to be a solid basis for society, no longer stand firm when rapidly confronted with other ways of thinking and other traditions. A sense of painful uncertainty takes over, a suffering that all of humanity more or less feels, and will certainly feel, as world civilizations and cultures are shaken by the impact of encountering whole groups of people who are different and previously unknown.

Why is this? The uncertainty comes from the fact that the mental structures of the Western world are, for the most part, intimately connected with the absolute values contained in these structures and expressed by them (such as ethics, aesthetics, metaphysics, freedom, justice, etc.). These values seem to be compromised when they come into contact with other mentalities and cultures. [...]

The fact is that absolute truths and values, such as eternal Truth, that is, the Kingdom of God, should not be confused with our own limited mental structures that contain them like a shell. The various and changing ideas and theories that are proposed today, and the uncertainty they cause, should not lead us to believe that the absolute values are being compromised. It might seem that these theories and constructs are so tied up with the truths they express that they are the same thing. But this is not true.

Attempts at a solution

Nonetheless, in this new situation, we find a growing uncertainty and uneasiness in people who are trying to protect themselves from this ideological earthquake, seeking shelter in one way or another.

Some are frightened and anchor themselves to what they know, and want to die in peace, leaving to future generations the task of solving the problem.

There are those who trust in their own strength and go out to discover a new civilization, new ideas or even other religions, believing they will find the answer in a synthesis of them all. [...] What happens then is a confusion of ideas that offer nothing valid or solid or absolute, and thus collapse into the most absurd and destructive relativism, in which everything is subjective.

Others would like to speed up the destruction of the old world, almost as if the birth of a new world will necessarily follow the demise of the present one.

Still others don't want to inconvenience themselves too much with thinking about it and so they leave to others the task of generating a new world, flinging themselves into a lifestyle of blind pragmatism [...]

And so, how can we live in the terrible situation we find today, in which it seems that a mysterious catastrophe is causing all our highest values to tremble and fall, like huge skyscrapers that bend over and break into pieces?

The world-person: Jesus Forsaken

Is there a practical answer [...], a sure way that can be trusted in order to work with others to generate the world of the future?

In reality, is there such a thing as a "global-person" who felt in himself this terrible earthquake, which is threatening to destroy everything that up until now was thought to be invulnerable? Is there someone who came to the point of almost doubting that the absolute truth itself was abandoning him to his own destiny, thus throwing him into a state of great confusion, and yet was able to overcome this terrible trial, paying for a new world, which he found anew within himself and generated for others?

Yes, such a person does exist.

But it is easy to understand this person couldn't be merely a human being, but had to be *the* human being: Jesus Forsaken. [...]

On the cross, close to his physical death and his mystical death in the abandonment, Jesus experienced the total collapse of his humanity, of his being human. We could say that he experienced the disintegration of his life as a human being. At that moment, the Father mysteriously permitted him to doubt that even God's presence in him had vanished. For this reason, he cried out, "My God, my God why have you forsaken me?"

But since he is God, precisely in this cry, Jesus had the strength to overcome this infinite suffering. He gives his mortal flesh the power of immortality, inserting his risen body into the heart of the immortal Trinity.

Not only, but with this extraordinary act of accepting the most horrible destruction ever known in heaven or on earth, Jesus gives humankind the possibility of rising again in the next life, with the resurrection of the flesh and also in this life, with a spiritual resurrection from any kind of death or destruction in which people could find themselves. [...]

He offers those who love him and follow him the Spirit of Truth, just as after his abandonment on Calvary he made the Holy Spirit descend upon the apostles.

When the Gen follow him, they will find the strength not to fear any situation, but rather to face it with the certainty that every human truth, and the Kingdom of Heaven which is the Truth, can find, also with their help, new mental structures on a worldwide level.

Furthermore, the Gen know that Christ lives in his Church, which was able to face all the events of history throughout the centuries, gradually stripping off customs, rituals and particular methods in order to hold firm to the truth that never changes. The recent Second Vatican Council is a luminous example of this effort of updating and renewal.

Therefore, remain firmly united to the Church and follow Jesus Forsaken.

It's up to you, Gen, to get to know him profoundly, to re-live him and to give a decisive and indispensable launch to the change that humanity needs to make.

It's up to you to welcome him in your hearts as the most precious pearl that could possibly be given to you today.

3. Church, a Community in Dialogue

In her book, *The Cry*, Chiara examines not only the sufferings of the Church in the light of Jesus Forsaken, but also what constitutes the Church as God's people, in other words, the institutional and charismatic dimensions, the Word of God and the sacraments.[124] She looks further and sees that Jesus in his abandonment is the key to know how to "go out" as Pope Francis says, to carry out concrete service to a wounded humanity through evangelization, but also by means of a 360-degree dialogue. In the following section, we look at this dimension which is a burning issue today, starting with a brief comment about the exercise of ministry and charisms.

In the Church that cries out

From the book, *The Cry*[125]

Jesus, in today's Church, cries out,
calling upon the divine to shine forth
and bring this earth to life;
calling for a re-establishment of the moral
order that can save the human race from ruin;
calling for our faith to be reaffirmed more

beautifully, more truly, freed from the non-
essential;
calling for social structures to be Christianized;
calling for all the faithful to be Church in its
deeper, etymological sense, which is communion,
"assembly";
calling for priests to be a light for the world;
and calling for bishops to work together with the
Pope to make unity shine more brightly (which is
not uniformity, but unity in diversity).
This is the Church to which our movement belongs
and to which it brings those divine jewels God
has placed in it, as in a vessel of clay.

Ministry and charisms today

From a talk given to 7,000 priests, religious and
seminarians at the Paul VI Hall

Vatican City, April 30, 1982[126]
We could say that this is the age of dialogue. We
are all called to dialogue, and priests, who have the
mission of evangelizing, are deeply involved in it. The
priest today has to be "a man of dialogue." [...]

But who is Jesus Crucified and Forsaken if not the
one who opened up the way to universal dialogue?
Wasn't it at the culmination of his passion,[127] in that
total exterior and interior annihilation,[128] that he
fulfilled his role as mediator between human beings
and God? Is it not there on the cross that he presents

himself to the Father as priest and victim for all humanity? [...]

Isn't that divine spiritual wound that opened in his heart, when even heaven closed itself to him, a wide open door through which human beings can finally unite themselves to God and God to them?

And since human beings, through Jesus Crucified, were able to restore a dialogue with God, a dialogue among them was also born. Jesus Crucified is the bond of unity also among human beings. [...]

Jesus Crucified and Forsaken. Who could ever sing his poverty, take on his obedience, measure his patience, reach his humility? Who knows his strength? Who could imagine his trust? Who could discern the abyss of his mercy or imitate his magnanimity? Who can love with his love?

In his light, many men and women religious rediscover the essence of the charism of their religious families. They understand the gift that God has given them, and find a new, filial love for their founders, with the desire to understand from them what is God's will for them. Having found their religious Father or Mother anew, they feel they are all brothers and sisters; they read the Rule with new eyes and deepen their unity with their superiors. A new profound unity is born, one filled with gratitude, unity with the hierarchy and, in particular, with the Holy Father, who because of his charism, takes in all the charisms of the Church.

Thus, Jesus and the Church are better served today also through the religious orders.

A way for every kind of dialogue

From a talk to people working in parishes and dioceses

Castel Gandolfo, Italy, April 20, 2002[129]

Now, from all that has been said, we can understand that Jesus Forsaken, having achieved unity in himself, having reunited heaven and earth, and people with one another, accomplished the most difficult and important dialogue, a dialogue which only he could have accomplished.

He was able to do it because he is Love, the greatest Love. He loved to the point of being reduced to this extent, to being crucified and abandoned by the Father, out of love for us.

He had already done it by being born on this earth, by becoming one of us, as love requires. He became a man, the "Son of Man," as he liked to call himself.

In assuming human nature, he took upon himself all that concerned it: our pain, our limitations, our faults. He even made himself "sin," as Paul says, even though he never sinned, and "excommunication," even though he was never excommunicated.

And all this because the Father had weighed him down with our burdens, with our problems, which he willingly accepted, and had asked him to make amends.

He became the master of love by emptying himself completely, reducing himself to nothing, losing even the sense of being the Son of God, God himself, in order to make us the children of God.

By doing so, he showed us the meaning of dialogue and what it demands for those who practice it.

The ecumenical Jesus Crucified

On several occasions, Chiara spoke of Jesus Forsaken as the "ecumenical Jesus Crucified." "In him lies the secret of the re-assembling of all Christian brothers and sisters in the full, visible communion that Christ had in mind." [130] It is an experience, albeit on a journey, which started with the first contacts with evangelical Lutheran Christians in Germany in the early 60s.

From a talk given to 7,000 priests, religious and seminarians at the Paul VI Hall

Vatican City, April 30, 1982[131]

The Work of Mary[132] does not belong only to the Catholic world. Mary brought it to life for Christians of other Churches as well. Together we form one reality, even with the limits that the still-existing divisions involve. Nevertheless, in our profound unity, we can see foreshadowed in a certain way what will come in the future.

Who urges all the Christian members of the movement to dialogue with one another, to foster, day by day, the communion among them which is already possible, to establish among all the presence of Jesus that our common baptism guarantees? Who urges Catholic priests to be united, as much as possible, with priests and ministers of other traditions?

It is Jesus Crucified who, in his cry of abandonment, took upon himself all the divisions of the world, all the consequences of our sin.

It is because of Jesus Crucified that we search out one another, that we love one another and that we hope, and do not give up, even when the endeavor seems arduous.

He, who, at the heart of history, paid for every division in the world, including the division among us Christians, has not yet seen the full fruits of his immense suffering.

Thus, it is he who spurs us on to sow, even though we will not be the ones to reap. It is he who urges us to look at the good of the Church, which will continue on after us; he who convinces us that if no one begins, and perseveres, no one will conclude.

Bonds with other religions

Surprisingly, Jesus Crucified can also be the meeting point with members of other religions, provided that the dialogue does not take place merely as a comparison of concepts and beliefs, but in the context of a living experience made of mutual listening and acceptance.

From a talk to Buddhist men and women monks and lay persons

Chiang Mai, Thailand, January 7, 1997[133]

This dialogue began not only among people of different churches, but also of different religions, and also with all men and women of good will.

Universal brotherhood is, in fact, the goal that we hope to reach through our love and mutual benevolence. We want to aim at a more united world.

However, one way to be able to reach unity is, for us Christians, the contemplation of a particular moment in the life of Jesus. I am referring to his abandonment, his total *kenosis* [emptying out of self] achieved on the cross out of love for his Father and for all humanity, the moment he precipitated into nothingness and cried out, "My God, my God, why have you forsaken me?"

He had lost everything, he was detached from everything. [...] It seemed to him that the Father himself had abandoned him. Therefore, he was reduced to nothing. And because of being reduced to nothing, he became the mediator between God and humanity, and of people with one another.

Then we know that he rose from the dead.

As we expanded all over the world, we met many faithful of other religions (Buddhists, Hindus, Sikhs, Muslims, Jews) and often it was Jesus in his abandonment who became the bond between ourselves and them.

In fact, it is often the practice in these religions to reach the goal of total denial of self and of one's instincts, with the consequent detachment from self, from other persons and from material things. In this way one aims at perfection.

Therefore, it is exactly when, on their part, they consider the mysterious pain of Jesus Forsaken and when, on our part, we consider their efforts to reach a state of nothingness, that a profound dialogue often opens up among us.

Once this dialogue has been thrown wide open, it offers us the possibility of finding in these religions many other values that are similar to what we, too, have to live in following our religion.

Jesus Crucified for the atheists

From the book, *The Cry*[134]

Turning our thoughts back to our brothers and sisters who profess no religious faith, we are convinced that the meaning of the Crucified Jesus we should present to them is not the meaning that was presented to the so-called pagans in the first centuries of the Church. For these brothers and sisters of ours today, salvation is not important, neither is resurrection nor the future world.

We need to present them with a *Crucified Jesus who seems to be only a man*. And that is how he appears in his forsakenness.

Furthermore, they need to meet Christians who love them so much that they are able, if one may say so, to experience the loss of God for the sake of others, like Jesus Forsaken. They need to see Christians who, like living crucifixes, know how to become, as Paul says, "as one outside the law" (1 Cor 9:21), in order to save one's brothers and sisters.

Gradually, these brothers and sisters of ours will begin to appreciate these people who are fulfilled persons, and yet have a certain simplicity. Appreciation leads to conversation, conversation to communion. Without realizing it, a divine dimension will enter their souls, and society, which, if at times is not built in God's name, can become his home, just like the pagan temples, at the onset of Christianity, became churches.

Jesus in his forsakenness is their Jesus Crucified, because, as we have seen, for them he made himself "atheist."

4. "Guarantee" for the Family

Jesus is true man as well as God. In him, and especially in the gift of his life to the point of the abandonment, the deeper meaning and ultimate foundation of our existence is revealed to us. Starting from him, all human realities can be renewed, and first of all, the family, the basic cell of society. In him, every fragility is accepted and healed.

The first spouse

An answer given to a young engaged woman

Ala di Stura, Italy, July 18, 1963[135]

You have said that your only good is Jesus. I feel called to marriage. Can I consecrate myself to him, too?

Not only can you, but you must! I'll explain why. In this world, things are not always done well. For example, many times the family has taken the place of God. The idea of forming a family is the ideal, the husband is the center and ideal for the wife, and the wife for the husband. This is not how it was among the first Christians. Jesus had just passed through the world and had left such a great sense of the divine that for the first Christians it was indifferent whether they married or didn't marry. If they decided to get married, they did it, but with the desire to follow Jesus! They would go to the catacombs, and they would die as martyrs, many times with their whole family. Now it is no longer like that in the world, but thanks be to God, we can give our contribution to putting things back in the right perspective. [...]

For those who have met this way of life and have put God in the first place in their life, even marriage, beautiful and holy as it is, is not everything for them, just like the first Christians. Therefore, my answer to you is, "Go along this way if that's where you feel called. But never betray—and I say this for your own happiness—never betray the first spouse you met, Jesus Crucified and Forsaken."

Make of the family a small Church

From the talk at the congress entitled "The family and education"

Castel Gandolfo, Italy, May 2, 1987[136]

Jesus has to live in us. How can this happen? The Gospel taught us how to do it. [...]

By not allowing our "old" self to live, but rather the "new" self, by loving in a supernatural way, by always being "outside of ourselves"—as we say—by overcoming eventual obstacles with love for Jesus Crucified and Forsaken, by not living our own life, but living the life of others, by making ourselves one with them in everything except sin...These are all ways that tell us how Jesus can take over our life. Jesus who is present in our souls through grace is more fully present when we correspond to that grace.

Yes, living in this way, Jesus is in us, Jesus the Teacher.

And yet, Jesus also has to live in our midst, within our families. [...]

We should make of our family [...] a little church and this means to model it on the family of Nazareth, that family which lived in such a concrete and yet divine way, with Jesus present in its midst. To accomplish this masterpiece, each member of the Holy Family loved each of the others in a supernatural way, and therefore, for God and not for themselves.

Mary, who was truly the mother of Jesus and truly the spouse of Joseph, loved both of them not for herself, but for God. And Joseph did not love Mary for himself; he loved her for God, just as he loved the Child Jesus for God, even though he was his adoptive father.

Yes, to love for God. And our love is truly purified from human attachments if our spirit is directed always towards Jesus Forsaken.

In his "why" find the answer to every cry

From a talk to the 19th international congress of the Swiss Foundation for the Family

Lucern, Switzerland, May 16, 1999[137]

The cry of every human being finds an answer in his cry, when he asked "why," but obtained no answer.

Isn't the person in anguish, or alone, or a failure, or condemned similar to him? Isn't every division within a family or among groups or among nations an image of him? Isn't the person who loses, so to say, the sense of God and of his plan for humanity, who no longer believes in love and accepts any kind of surrogate in its place, a figure of Jesus Forsaken? There is no human tragedy or family failure that is not contained in that "night" of the Man-God. With that kind of death, he already paid for everything. He signed a blank check which covered all the suffering and all the sin of humanity that has been, is and will be.

In that terrible experience, he was the divine grain of wheat that rots and dies to give us back life. Thus he shows us the truth about the greatest possible love, which is to be capable of giving all of oneself, to become nothing for others. [...]

Through that emptiness, that nothingness, grace and the life of God flowed back to humanity. Christ reestablished the unity between God and creation, he restored the design, he made new men and new women and, therefore, also new families.

The great event of the suffering and abandonment of the God-Man can, therefore, become the reference point and the secret wellspring capable of transforming death into resurrection, limitations into opportunities to love, family crises into stages of growth. How?

If we look at suffering from a purely human perspective, there are two possibilities. We either end up in an analysis that has no way out, since suffering and love are part of the mystery of human life, or we try to rid ourselves of this uncomfortable obstacle by running in the opposite direction.

But if we believe that behind the events of our life there is God with his love, then, strengthened by this faith, we can recognize in the small or big daily sufferings of our own or of others, a shadow of the Crucified and Forsaken Christ. We will see that suffering is our participation in the pain that redeemed the world, and it will be possible to understand the meaning of even the most absurd situations and put them in perspective.

When confronted with any suffering, whether large or small, and all the contradictions of life and problems that have no solutions, let's try to enter within ourselves and face the absurdity, the injustice, the innocent suffering, the humiliation, the alienation, the desperation...and we will recognize in them one of the many countenances of the "Man of Sorrows."

It will be a meeting with him, the divine Person who became an individual without relationships, a meeting with the God of contemporary man, who changes "nothingness" into "being," and suffering into love. It will be our "yes" to him, our readiness to love him and welcome him into our lives that will cause our individualistic attitudes to crumble and turn us into new men and new women who through love are capable of healing and giving new life to the most desperate situations.

5. Our Key Idea

God sees the world[138] through the "pupil" of the wound of the abandonment, which also unfolds for us a totally different vision of things. It is a vision that goes to the root of the issues and sheds light on how to read and deal with challenges, creating a new style, a new mentality, a new way of acting. Because the Spirit of God was poured out on humankind from the wound of Jesus Forsaken, it is from him, from the relationship with him, that an innovative intelligence can spring forth, able to "flood" with light the various fields of culture, from politics to psychology, from philosophy to sociology[139], and renew them from within. By way of example, we consider now observations of Chiara regarding education, the arts and communication, which originated in close contact with the protagonists in each of these fields.

Educating to face difficulties

From a talk given during the conferral of an honorary doctorate in education

Washington, DC, November 10, 2000[140]

Jesus Forsaken is our secret, a key idea for us in the field of education, too. He indicates the "limitless" quality of our work as educators, demonstrating to us how far we need to go and what ardent commitment we need to have in educating others.

But who is this Jesus Forsaken whom we have decided to love in a preferential way? He is the figure of those who are ignorant (his ignorance is the most tragic, his question the most dramatic). He is the figure of all who are needy, or maladjusted, or disabled; of those who are unloved, neglected, or excluded. He personifies all those human and social situations, which, more than any others, have an urgent and particular need for education.

Jesus Forsaken represents all those who lack everything and therefore, need someone to give them everything and do everything for them. He is the model of someone who needs to learn and therefore solicits the responsibility of the teacher. Jesus Forsaken shows us the limitless need for education, and at the same time, the limitless responsibility of educators.

However, Jesus Forsaken went beyond his own infinite suffering and prayed, "Father, into your hands I commend my spirit" (Lk 23:46). And so, he also teaches us to see difficulties, obstacles, trials, hard work, error, failure and suffering as something that must be faced, loved and overcome. Generally, we human beings, whatever our field of endeavor, seek to avoid such experiences in every possible way.

In the field of education as well, there is often a tendency to be overprotective with young people, shielding them from all that is difficult, teaching them to view the road of life as smooth and comfortable. In reality, this leaves them extremely unprepared to face the inevitable trials of life. In particular, it fosters passivity and a reluctance to accept responsibility for oneself, for one's neighbor and for society in general, as every mature human being should.

For us, instead, precisely because of our choice of Jesus Forsaken, every difficulty should be faced and loved. And thus, educating children to face difficulties, which involves commitment on the part of both the educator and the one being educated, is another key idea in our educational method.

Model for artists

From an address to the International Congress of Artists

Castel Gandolfo, Italy, April 23, 1999[141]

Jesus Forsaken on the cross was certainly not beautiful.

In fact, the Word of God, the Great Artist, became incarnate and assumed our human nature to the point of making himself sin, though never a sinner. "He had no form or majesty," says Isaiah, "that we should look at him, nothing in his appearance that we should desire him" (Is 53:2). And yet our faith tells us that in him the glory of the resurrection was already present.

Jesus Crucified and Forsaken is the model of artists and especially of the artists in our movement, who, like him, will always know how to offer, even in the saddest circumstances, a ray of hope. The Holy Father told artists: "All great artists confront, at times throughout their lives, the problem of suffering and despair. Nonetheless, many have let hope shine through their work, hope that is greater than suffering and decadence. Expressing themselves in literature, or in music, in molding materials or in painting they have evoked the mystery of a new salvation, of a world renewed. In our times, too, this has to be the message of genuine artists, who live with sincerity all that is human, even human tragedy, but know with precision how to reveal, in tragedy itself, the hope that has been given to us." [142]

At the root of communication

Response to a question during a convention for people involved in various ways in the field of communications and the media

Castel Gandolfo, Italy, June 2, 2000[143]
"What is the basis for communication that enriches and unites humanity, and how do we achieve it?"

I am not an expert in the media, as I am not in many other fields, but I would reply with St. Paul: "For I decided to know nothing among you except Jesus Christ, and him crucified" (1 Cor 2:2). I would add to this, "crucified and forsaken," according to the particular aspect of Jesus' passion that has become part of our spirituality. [...]

Jesus ended his earthly existence by being put to death in the most shameful way possible for his day (crucifixion, reserved for slaves), a punishment that also meant separation from the community, total rejection, elimination of any social and religious affiliation for the condemned person.

The "great communicator," who had captivated the crowds, now found himself alone, betrayed, ignored. His chief disciple claimed, "I do not know this man" (Mk 14:71)

But that was not all. Even God the Father, who, as Jesus had proclaimed, knows all that is hidden (cf. Jn 5:20) and whose relationship had always supported him, broke off all communication. This "abandonment" is certainly the darkest night, the most dreadful agony and so he cries out, "My God, my God, why have you forsaken me?" (Mt 27:46).

His cry, which sums up the nothingness of all things, has always accompanied human history. We can cite here two images that certainly are fixed in all our memories. Who does not recall the agony of *The Scream*, the painting by the Norwegian, Edvard Munch, symbol of the isolation of a human being without relationships? Or the terror caught by a reporter's casual snapshot of the little Vietnamese girl, Kim Phuc, wrapped in napalm flames as she fled screaming from her scorched town, the very image of humanity in a child torn from her roots?

These appalling signs draw us back to the abyss of forsakenness experienced by Christ the Word who cries out at the silence, at the "absence" of God.

Jesus Crucified and Forsaken, the mediator (the medium, the channel) between humanity and God, who, when the final barrier collapses, when unity has been achieved, disappears and becomes nothing, is a frightful and yet fascinating mystery. He is an infinite void, almost the pupil of God's eye, window through which God can look at humanity and humanity in a certain way can see God.

He spoke, lived and worked, and taught for three years, and his words, spoken "for all time" were then and will be for all eternity "the way, and the truth, and the life" (Jn 14:6). Yet our faith teaches us that his being "himself" reached fulfillment at the moment of his most total gift, when he offered his life in the way just described.

So we can ask ourselves, was his cry at the ninth hour his fullest expression as "the Word"? Was it, so to speak, the height of his communication?

Yes. And it is in this self-annihilation, in the abyss of individuality, where every relationship is dead, that he gives us the gift of his reality *as person*, capable of encountering God and humanity.[144] Precisely in giving himself without limit he reveals himself as Word, infinitely communicating himself, introducing us into the mystery of redemption and the life of God, into the vortex of love among Father, Son and Holy Spirit.

Chapter 5

"The Holy Journey"
Striving for Holiness,
in Communion With Others

From the beginning of the adventure of unity, it was all a question of love: love as our response to Jesus in his greatest suffering, and love in our gift of self to others, out of love for him. It was a radical love that didn't allow for any self-centeredness, not even seeking one's own holiness. Much later, at the beginning of the 60s, after reading the writings of St. Teresa of Avila, Chiara discovered that we achieve holiness precisely in this way, that is, by loving.

The decades that followed were characterized by considerable development of the Focolare Movement, which expanded into a variety of fields. And yet in Chiara's soul everything was always a question of uncompromising love. She constantly refined her own self-giving and asked others to do the same, making it full and pure, with no ulterior motives. She continually deepened her relationship with Jesus Forsaken, suggesting new ways to love him. She strove tenaciously to reach sanctity, so as to be a transparent witness to her Ideal, God.

In the early 80s, she began the "Holy Journey," united together with all those who follow the path of unity. Among other things, the international conference calls that took place throughout the world served this purpose. She could not conceive of holiness unless it was shared with others. In fact, she proposed the "sanctity of the people." Jesus Forsaken was and always remains the primary guide and constant point of reference in this process.

I have to become a saint

From a page of her diary

Rocca di Papa, Italy, May 10, 1991[145]

The idea that dominates my soul is "I have to become a saint."

This is because I have to leave something more to those who follow me—my sanctity. It's necessary that they have a model, which is more valuable that many written words.

I have aimed at sanctity my whole life, and so it shouldn't be too difficult. And it would be a pity if I don't conclude it well.

This morning I understood once again that my sanctity is Jesus Forsaken. He attracts me like a magnet in this last period, just like [Mary] the Desolate has a special fascination for me.

I'm attracted by their "nothingness." That's where sanctity lies—the nothingness of ourselves so that God triumphs in us. I find this nothingness by loving his will and loving my neighbors, but also by "losing" everything that needs to be lost, immediately and with generosity.

This is what I will try to do.

Maybe I'll get there in time.

1. If You Don't Love Me, Who Will?

For Chiara, Christian life was summarized in a dynamic "one-on-one" relationship with God, nothing less than a "marriage," with all this entails: passionate love, fidelity and daily attention to the one who first loved us (cf Rm 5:8; 1 Jn 4:10). It is a reality to be carried out tirelessly and uncompromisingly.

For twenty centuries

From a talk on "Jesus Forsaken and life"

October 3, 2005[146]

Throughout my life, I often thought that death was close. Years ago, however, this thought left me in turmoil. I felt that if God had called me so soon to himself, I would not be able to present myself to him with the sanctity that he expected of me.

Therefore, I asked him to give me a push, a decisive push, and he indicated to me Jesus Forsaken as my one and only way. Wasn't he the one who had given us such a strong impulse at the very beginning of the movement? The Lord was inviting me to conclude my life as I had started it, making it a race to love only him forsaken.

In those days, in 1980, I felt that Jesus Forsaken himself was telling me, "If you don't love me, who will?" It seemed he was telling me that he, Jesus Forsaken, had revealed himself to me first of all, as if for twenty centuries he had been aiming at me.

Following this experience, the whole movement set off on what we called the "Holy Journey." And in the subsequent years, we had the joy of seeing numerous members of the movement leave for heaven seemingly as saints. For several, the process of beatification has already begun. These brothers and sisters of ours have reached the goal, and they are the prelude of that crowd of saints that our charism wants to form for the honor and glory of Mary.

I cannot divorce him

Pages from her diary

August 15, 1970[147]

I meditated on the fact of how true it is that I have only one Spouse on earth, Jesus Forsaken, and that I cannot divorce him by choosing something that is not suffering, darkness, agony, anguish, desperation, etc. In the same way I cannot disown the only mother I have, Mary Desolate, who held

Jesus dead in her lap and offered him to the Father without a lament.

December 12, 1971[148]

I have a great desire to read the Song of Songs. Maybe I will find something there for me in this moment.

And yet, Jesus, "for me" is not important. Help the focolarini. Maintain, enkindle or reinkindle their love, their falling in love with you, something many of them have experienced.

I have had more than enough graces. [...]

One doesn't touch certain peaks without the danger of falling into the precipice; one doesn't receive certain graces without the danger that—if they are neglected—life finishes badly, both here and there.

You don't marry Jesus Forsaken forever with your whole heart and all the strength you have, and then leave him one disastrous day, [...] divorcing him and marrying someone or something else.

God is jealous. [...]

If we have married him, we have to be faithful in every moment.

Every day has 24 hours

From a page in her diary

December 30, 1971[149]

In these days, I feel always more my call to suffering, to Jesus Forsaken. My fear is that I will forget that! And so I think about the fact that every day has 24 hours and that all I have to do is remember him in these few hours of every day.

And also to remember to look for him with joy in his will in each moment and to always be waiting for him when he comes.

Today every time I look at my watch, I will remember that it's time to love Jesus Forsaken.

From a page in her diary, then shared in an international conference call

Mollens, Switzerland, September 17, 1980[150]

I realized with terror that a whole day passed without my remembering Jesus Forsaken, except when I said the rosary. That's terrible! My life is slipping away day by day and I have to present myself at the meeting with Jesus, giving an account of how much I loved him forsaken. Haven't I married him? And does any spouse forget her husband for a whole day?

I think that my failure is due to the fact that the days spent up here [in Switzerland] are so full of spiritual joys. Obviously, it's a period like this, but I feel afraid without him. He is the sum total of sanctity, he is the supreme teacher of the spiritual life, of detachment from ourselves, from other people, from everything, from what is of God but is not God.

He is the yardstick on which I have to measure myself to know how to love all the neighbors I meet during the day. He is the one and only guarantee of my union with him and of the true and real unity among us. Living with him I will certainly be a saint and, like him, the mother of many souls.

With him I have everything. Without him, I am no longer myself. I asked him to forgive me and I'm starting over again.

Compete with him in fidelity

From an international conference call message

May 20, 1982[151]

Something that never ceases to amaze me and that moves me when I see it in our lives, is the fidelity of Jesus Forsaken. He has made himself so one with everyone, being the first to practice the art of loving in such a sublime and heroic degree, that every person on earth can feel he is close to them in every difficulty, and especially in moments of suffering.

Do we feel forsaken or alone? He is there. Betrayed or humiliated? He is there, too. Do we feel lukewarm, disoriented, excluded? Failures or sinners? He is there. He is always faithful. He never fails to be there. In fact, just when everyone else disappears, that is the moment when he appears.

Well, then, let this be our resolution for the next two weeks: *to compete with him in being faithful.* Let's be wherever he is, unwavering, ready to love him, to embrace him.

Is he there in some personal sufferings we have? Then let's be there with him.

Is he in our family, which is suffering, in our community, which is lacking the sunshine of love, of unity? Let's be there.

Is he in the divisions among Christians? Let's be there on the front lines! Is he in those who do not know the true faith? Let's be there, too. Is he in our cold, atheistic or secularistic environment? Let's be there, too, to embrace him in that coldness.

My whole heart for him

Excerpts from her diary

October 7, 1983[152]

Today: "I have *only one* Spouse on earth." Therefore, to love only, or better, above all, suffering. I will no longer complain about anything that represents my Spouse. A true spouse loves her husband above all else. It's true that she will also love her mother and her other relatives, but she married only one. So, I, too, will love the joy that Jesus in our midst gives me and other joys [...], but my heart will be first of all for him.

October 23, 1983[153]

Even on good days, as far as my health is concerned, I should not forget Jesus Forsaken because I have only one Spouse. I did not marry my health, or feeling good, or delighting in the joys that the movement gives, but rather I married him. And if I do not have any sufferings, I have to meet him by practising the virtues with constancy. For example, patience, mercy, heroic charity [...].

And so today, that's what I will do: look for him. If I am attentive and listen to "that little voice," he will give me many opportunities to show him my love.

2. The Death of Our Ego

The "way to unity" aims at the positive: charity. But its roots are found in the "negative" virtues, which Chiara sees as the "daughters of love," love's pillars and guarantee. They prevent selfishness in its various forms from prevailing in us. Jesus, Love, cannot live in us without the simultaneous death of our "ego." In this way, our true personality, the one that we always had in God, emerges.

Detached from everything

From a page of her diary

Zurich, Switzerland, March 23, 1981[154]

I am attracted to that "detachment" from everything that is not the will of God, because detachment *is* Jesus Forsaken.

I am certain that every detachment is a little pruning and so I await, for his glory, a blossoming of life.

And I am happy that this new love for "detachment" came to me during Lent, so I am in harmony with the Church, my Mother and his Spouse.

I notice that this aspect of Jesus Forsaken has always been present in our story, right from the beginning, when we used to say, "Because you are forsaken…"

At the time, we were sleeping on some mattresses on the floor and in front of us, on the wall, was his Face to signify that, from then on (and that's what we wanted with our whole heart), we had only one love, which was him.

Then we found him, above all, in every suffering, while it became ever clearer to us that charity was our path, charity that brings about unity, charity that is the mother of all virtues and animates them. [...]

From those early days, we used to say, "Not just denying ourselves, but being dead." It was Jesus Forsaken who became sin, making himself nothing, who suggested this sentence to us. He was our *nada*, our "nothing."

Then we learned to prefer him, to cohabitate with him, to celebrate when he came, meaning that it was always him in sufferings and also in the various ways to practice self-denial.

There was also the glorious moment of discovering Mary Desolate, who presented herself to us in all the splendor of her virtues, inviting us to imitate her.

This was where the idea of "losing" came about, "knowing how to lose," especially in the present moment, all that is not the will of God. And our decision to say, "I have only one Mother on earth..."

Then there were the "various clothes" of Jesus Forsaken, which referred to the various aspects of his suffering. [...]

At another point we tried to be detached from those things in our life that were the "appetites" [desires] described by St. John of the Cross. [...]

May Jesus Forsaken teach us to lose everthing that is not God. A life in the midst of the world, like the one we have, and an ideal of unity, that brings us to make ourselves one with everyone, is full of dangers, if you don't have in your heart a very radical ideal.

Jesus Forsaken will help us.

March 27, 1981[155]

Today repeat all day long, "Because you are Forsaken." Repeat it in embracing "always, immediately and with joy" the crosses that come, the detachments required by the will of God, the self-denial of Lent, the meeting with persons who are similar to him, or when problems come (he asked "why?") or doubts, or when I have to "lose" my own will in the present moment.

March 28, 1981[156]

It's indescribable what I experienced yesterday by living like this. It's a secret joy, an emotion of the soul, but, above all, a very profound sensation, of a supernatural kind, of having found my way, the path for my life.

This is my vocation: Jesus Forsaken.

I can, I must repeat, "I have only one Spouse on earth, I have no other God but him."

Yes, I don't have another way; there is no alternative, no other life, no other star, no other heaven, no other love outside of him.

"Jumping like a kangaroo"[157] *and "bombarding"*

From an international conference call

May 20, 1982[158]

Jesus Forsaken is our whole life. Every act of love for him gives a new thrust to our holy journey, a tonic for our soul. And we feel like saying that the Gospel is really right when it says, "Those who lose their life for my sake will save it" (Lk. 9:24). It is really by dying that we live. This is our experience every day, every hour.

When we don't live this way, when we don't say "no" to our ego by denying ourselves and leaping out of our will into God's will, like the kangaroos [who only leap forward], when we don't deny our ego in order to make ourselves one with our neighbor, then we have the impression that we are not living. Rather—how can I put it?—we are just vegetating.

From an international conference call

October 1, 1981[159]

And so, we return to the idea of "cutting," "bombarding," giving up, doing away with, "declaring war" on everything that is not him, that is not his will in the present moment. This is what we have to do! Let's love Jesus Forsaken, who is hiding behind this cutting and losing, as our one and only love.

Toward the life that does not die

From a page of her diary shared during an international conference call

London, June 14, 1981[160]
I will love today the suffering of detachments required by the will of God during this day of rest. I will turn the page with determination, with a jump into the new will of God out of love for Jesus Forsaken, ready, if he comes, to embrace him always, immediately and with joy.

In this way, if I live dying, I will die, at my hour, living the Life that does not die.

And I know now how alive this death is, how full this solitude, how much light there is in this darkness.

"I have set about dying"

From an international conference call

Rocca di Papa, Italy, November 3, 1983[161]
Which Jesus Forsaken do we have to embrace in each present moment? The one required by our life as Christians, which is self-denial and taking up our own cross, in order to follow Jesus.

Therefore, we need to say "yes" to Jesus Forsaken and quickly embrace every suffering that comes our way—in other words, our cross. But in order for love to triumph in our hearts, we also need to embrace the suffering that comes from our efforts to deny ourselves, and from the struggle against our selfishness and the so-called desires of the flesh (tendencies toward overeating, impurity, quarreling, jealousy, and so on).

If, in the present moment, these efforts are loved out of love for Jesus Crucified and if, immediately afterwards, we do what God wants from us in that moment, we can experience the fullness of the life of the Risen Lord, even when we are alone. Then his light comes into our hearts. His peace fills us. His love is enkindled in us, and with it, consolation, serenity, a taste of heaven. In other words, everything changes. The soul is clothed in newness...[...]

When Igino Giordani[162] wrote the following poem, shortly after he had embraced our spirituality, that's precisely what he meant:

"I have resolved to die
and what happens no longer matters to me.
I have begun to find my joy
in Jesus' desolate heart."[163]

He was speaking of dying to self, so as to rejoice with Jesus, of dying with the Forsaken Jesus, so as to live with the Risen Jesus.

So let's remember these words: "I have resolved to die." And let's welcome the death of our own self, ten times, a hundred times a day, so as to give those we meet the joy of encountering the Risen Lord.

3. Nurturing the Life of Jesus in Us

The "way of unity" has many facets. It is complex, but not complicated; rather it is simple, like life. By pointing in only one direction, which is to love Love, to love the abandoned Christ, it points to the very center of Christian life, and everything else comes as a consequence. It is for this reason that Chiara taught people to nurture the virtues, as a way to demonstrate their unique and exclusive choice of Jesus Forsaken.

Set the compass on the goal

From a message to the "Volunteers of God" [164] at Mariapolis Foco (Montet, Switzerland)

August 6, 1981[165]

I remember a trip I took many years ago. I was on a plane and the pilot kindly invited me into the cabin to see the splendid panorama. Then he told me, more or less, "Do you see how easy it is to fly a plane? All you have to do is set the compass exactly on the point where you want to go and be careful it doesn't move from there." I understood that the hard parts were the take-off and the landing. For the rest, you just have to watch the compass.

So I thought, "Just like life!" [...] It's hard to take off, because you have to leave everything else aside. "Whoever does not leave..." And it's hard to land in the next life. In fact those last moments are very difficult. For all the rest, the only thing you have to do is keep the needle of the compass of life fixed on just one point—Jesus Forsaken—and be careful that it never moves from there. That's exactly the way it is! With the eyes of our soul fixed on Jesus Forsaken, we have union with God, a deeper union with others, perfect self-renunciation and, little by little, we gain all the virtues. What more could we want?

And so? "You know, Jesus Forsaken, that to love you I only have now." Love him in the crosses that come, always, immediately and with joy. Love him in others, especially those who are most similar to him. Love him in the Eucharist where he is present. And love him in the total renunciation of ourselves. Doing all of this, we will keep alive the resolve we need to have to give Mary one day the gift of our sanctity, for her glory and the glory of God.

From an international conference call

Rocca di Papa, January 5, 1984[166]

December 31, 1983 marked the third anniversary of our Holy Journey, and we asked ourselves, "How far have we gone?" We felt a very strong desire not to waste any more time.

I think I can say that setting the needle of our spiritual compass on Jesus Forsaken is the best possible step we can take to continue and complete our Holy Journey, and also to cover the distance remaining with a certain ease.

When I was on that plane, I had noticed that the pilot was very free in his movements, because he used no reins, as you would need with a horse; nor a steering wheel, as you would need in a car. Similarly, if we set the needle of our spiritual compass on Jesus Forsaken, we will not need anything else to reach the goal safely.

Just as in a plane there are no curves to take you by surprise, because you fly in a straight line, and you don't have the problem of mountains, because you quickly reach a high altitude, so too, on our Holy Journey, our love for Jesus Forsaken immediately places us on high. Thus we are not frightened by unforeseen circumstances, nor tired out by climbing, because in Jesus Forsaken, whatever is unforeseen, difficult or painful is already foreseen and expected.

So let's set our compass on Jesus Forsaken, and then let's remain faithful to him.

How? In the morning, as soon as we wake up, let's point the needle of our compass toward Jesus Forsaken, telling him, "Here I am!" Then, during the day, from time to time, let's check our compass and see if we're still on course with Jesus Forsaken. If we find we're not, then let's tell him again, "Here I am!" Then get back on the right course immediately and the journey will go ahead well.

Charity and the virtues

From a page of her diary

December 12, 1971[167]

Since in these days I have great joy in my heart, I am not waiting to choose him only when he comes to me, but I am choosing him in the present. Or better I want to choose him. For example, I am attracted to acts of self-denial.

It seems strange, but that's the way it is. I know that self-denial is him.

Perhaps I am attracted to practicing renunciation because of the law of opposites. Having lived (for better or worse) a life of charity, now I am attracted to the other virtues.

And as long as I have this grace, I will take advantage of it. And I see how much has to be done in this area!

Try it and you will see how "wild" we are and how many branches need to be cut, in every sense. Yes, in every sense and in all the senses, that is, in everything that has to do with our senses.

Always, immediately and with joy

From a page of her diary

December 30, 1980[168]

In order to declare someone a saint, the Church wants to see heroic virtue, which means that a person accepts immediately trials that are greater than human strength and do so happily, every time they come.

If we have Jesus Forsaken as the ideal of our life, we will reach the point of having this kind of virtue. In fact, his was a trial that was greater that any human strength and, on occasion, we will imitate him in this. And if we see only him, we will accept him every time he comes, immediately and with joy.

I shared this conviction of mine with a focolarino and he repeated to me a motto that did us a lot of good some years ago: "always, immediately and with joy."

That's how it is. This is the attitude we need to have. [...]

The only thing to do is to start loving Jesus Forsaken in ourselves, in others and in every event—always, immediately and with joy.

From a page of her diary shared during an international conference call

March 28, 1981[169]

Jesus Forsaken is for us the highest example of every virtue, which he lived out of love for God and us.

In that moment, every virtue shone out brilliantly: extreme poverty, complete humility, perseverance to the end, heroic trust, blind obedience, incarnate mercy, incredible strength, hope against every hope—every virtue.

The vineyard of Jesus Forsaken

From an international conference call

Sierre, Switzerland, January 20, 1983[170]

The Work of Mary is, as we know, the vineyard of Jesus Forsaken. And each of us individually is a vine, a vine alive with the Life that is Jesus, who said, "I am the life" (Jn 14:6)

I am always impressed, especially during the winter, when I see how the grapevines are culti-vated here in Valais, Switzerland. How much care is given to them, and what discipline they are sub-jected to!

They give excellent wine, that's true, but how much work they demand!

You see them lined up in perfectly straight rows, equidistant from one another, so that each one will be fully exposed to the sun.

You see how they are perfectly pruned of all the unnecessary branches, so that in some instances only one branch is left to bear its abundant fruit, its succulent bunches of grapes.

They are tied firmly to a stick so that they will stand straight and not drag on the ground.

All the ground around them is cleaned of the many leaves that fell during the harvest. If the vines are still very small, you see them surrounded by a circular net to protect them; and so on, with still other clever devices.

I thought of us, of the little vine of Jesus' life growing in us, and of the care that we should give it. We must, first of all, keep it in the sunlight, well-exposed to God's presence in prayer, when we converse with Jesus in our heart. We must keep it well-pruned of any unnecessary branches, that is, of all the activities that we would like to engage in, but which are not God's will for us.

We have to keep this life firmly bound to Jesus Forsaken, who enables us to love the suffering that comes upon us unexpectedly, as well as the suffering that self-denial entails.

We have to maintain the ground around our vine clean, keeping far away from us the things or persons that were a cause of temptation in our past life: unhealthy friendships, various little vices, television programs that it would be better not to watch, unnecessary possessions and things empty of true value…

And above all, if our grapevine is still small, we should protect it with the unity with those who share our spirituality […].

We need to spend the rest of our life cultivating Jesus' life in us, so that the immense vineyard of Jesus Forsaken throughout the world may grow and develop more and more and bring us closer to the *"ut omnes"* ("that they may all be one.")

4. "A Thousand Obstacles"

No matter what our commitment or how serious and sincere our choices may have been, our human shortcomings, sooner or later, always tend to surface at some point. They can drive us to think that we will never make it, or to resign ourselves to a "half-baked," mediocre life. Jesus Forsaken, instead, gives us the opportunity to make a springboard out of every obstacle. However, the communion with others is also important, making it easier to find together the adequate solution for the difficulties that we encounter, and to discern what help we may need along the way.

From a page of her diary

June 26, 1971[171]

"The way of love" that we speak about […] is long and has thousands of difficulties, thousands of obstacles, and whoever has not chosen the difficulty, the obstacle, the absurd, the temptation premitted by God, the "night," and everything else that speaks of suffering, and does not transform it into the positive, seeing the face of Jesus Forsaken to be loved, will undoubtedly give up. […]

May God keep a hand on our heads, because at any spiritual or physical age, we can do something foolish.

Perfectionism that is not love

From a page of her diary

October 30, 1983[172]

Even loving Jesus Forsaken can become a trap for our spiritual life and make us concentrate on ourselves, thinking that we have to be perfect, but in a way that is not love.

That's why we always have to keep in mind the other side of the coin, which is unity. Jesus Forsaken aims at unity. He did not love suffering in itself, but he *used* it—if we can use this word—to reunite humanity with God and with one another. We have to love him in order to have union with God, but for the sake of our neighbor.

When we embrace Jesus Forsaken, and he obtains for us the triumphal entry of God into our soul (with the gifts of the Holy Spirit), we need to pour out this love in abundance on our neighbors.

Overcoming discouragement

From an international conference call

Rocca di Papa, Italy, October 17, 1985[173]

As we know, in our Holy Journey we are aiming at sanctity. But we can only truly aim at sanctity if it is a goal that we definitely hope to achieve. [...]

All the same, there may be some among us who do not see it in this way. Perhaps because they think too much about their sins in the past, or about how slow they have been to correspond to the graces up to now. There is a danger, then, of becoming resigned to leading a mediocre life…

This is a serious mistake.

In whatever situation we may find ourselves at the moment, we have to be certain that we will make it. There are three reasons to be encouraged. First of all, there is this month's Word of Life: "For God all things are possible" (Mk 10:27). Secondly, there are the saints. In fact, those who have been canonized have not always been so saintly. Let's recall St. Jerome who, bowed down under the weight of his sins, heard the Lord tell him, "Give me your sins." Let's think of St. Augustine, of Blessed Angela of Foligno, of St. Ignatius of Loyola, of St. Teresa of Avila herself, who, even though she hadn't committed grave sins, throughout her whole lifetime felt the weight of her initial lack of response to God.

Then there is a third reason that gives us hope: our brothers and sisters who have recently completed their Holy Journey. In fact, many of them made it to the end, and the conclusion of their lives was stupendous. […]

But how can we reach such heights? Above all, every time we are overwhelmed by discouragement because it seems impossible for us to reach the goal of sanctity, instead of hesitating, we should tell Jesus that we thank him for his work in digging the foundations of humility in our souls, the necessary premise for sanctity. Tell him that we are happy because nothing is more important to us than to see ourselves in every moment of life similar to him forsaken. And assure him that we wouldn't exchange these moments with any other, because he is the one who is most important to us. He is the one we have chosen.

In this way, the Risen Lord takes hold within us and with him there is the certainty that, even though we may not be aware of it, he is drawing us away from a Christian life that might be tepid and bringing us into the spheres of his fire.

In front of an obstacle, call him by name
From an international conference call

August 28, 1986[174]

It is always a great discovery to see how we can, in a certain way, give the name "Jesus Forsaken" to every suffering and trial of life.

Are we overwhelmed by fear? Didn't Jesus on the cross in his abandonment seem to be overcome with the fear that the Father may have forgotten him? [...]

Do circumstances cause us to feel disoriented? In his tremendous suffering, Jesus seems not to understand anything of what is happening to him and cries out, "Why?" (cf. Mt 27:46; Mk 15:34).

Are we contradicted? Doesn't it seem in the abandonment that the Father doesn't approve of what Jesus is doing?

Have we been reprimanded, or been faced with accusations? On the cross, Jesus in his abandonment perhaps had the impression of being reprimanded, or being accused even by heaven.

And then, in certain trials in life that can follow one right after another, don't we sometimes even reach the point of saying, "This is all too much, this is beyond the limit"? In his abandonment, Jesus drank from a bitter chalice that was not only full, but overflowing. His trial was one that was beyond every limit.

And when we are surprised by disappointments, or wounded by a trauma, or by an unforeseen misfortune, or by an illness or an absurd situation, we can always recall the suffering of Jesus Forsaken who personified all these trials and thousands of others.

Yes, he is present in everything that can cause suffering. Each suffering is another name for him.

There is an expression used in the world, which says that you call your loved one by name. We have decided to love Jesus Forsaken. And so, to better succeed in doing that, let's get used to calling him by name in the various trials of our life.

We will call him: Jesus Forsaken-loneliness, Jesus Forsaken-doubt, Jesus Forsaken-injury, Jesus Forsaken-trial, Jesus Forsaken-desolation, and so forth.

And calling him by name, he will see that he is discovered and recognized under every suffering, and will respond to us with more love. By embracing him, he will become our peace, our comfort, our courage, our stability, our health and our victory. He will be the explanation for everything, the solution to everything.

With temptations, resist right from the beginning

From an international conference call

Rocca di Papa, April 23, 1987[175]

There is a surprising saying in the Scriptures: "Because you were acceptable to God, it was necessary that temptation should prove you" (Tb 12:13).[176]

It speaks about temptations and it says plainly that temptations come not only to people who are on the side of evil, but also to good people who are acceptable to God, and loved by him. [...]

The saints always had big and small trials, but they took advantage of them to make progress on the road to perfection, instead of stopping or going backward.

What about us? What is our typical attitude [...] when faced with temptation?

We always try to love: to love God by doing his will and to love our neighbor.

As long as we love, a temptation is sure to have a hard time working its way into our soul, because charity produces virtues, not vices. But it can happen, it's only human, that we are not always in a loving attitude. That's when a temptation, large or small, can surface more easily.

We have learned that the pain of temptation and the discomfort it brings to one who is trying to live a Christian life is one of many sufferings we can experience, one of many faces of Jesus Forsaken. We feel it's our duty then to embrace the pain and conquer it, plunging ourselves at once into living the next moment well.

That is what we should always do.

All the same, it is not good to trust solely in our own strength to overcome these trials. They can come often, and be prolonged, and even make us fall. It is then that we have to arm ourselves with patience and repeat constantly our efforts to conquer them, as often as necessary. But most of all, we have to trust in God, asking him in prayer for his indispensable aid.

The best and most necessary thing to do, however, in order to conquer temptations is to keep vigilant watch right from the start, as soon as they make an appearance, so as not to let them cross the threshold of our mind. Otherwise, the battle becomes much more difficult. There is a slogan, "Resist from the start," which for us means to embrace Jesus Forsaken immediately.

The one and only star

From an international conference call

August 27, 1987[177]

For us to choose Jesus Forsaken is indispensable. [...]

But is it easy to remain faithful to him? Yes, if the trials are small; no, if they are more substantial. In fact, at times it is by no means easy. Or better, it can be very hard and seem all but impossible.

Here at the central headquarters of the movement, we, too, very often hear about severe suffering [...], pain that tests the limits of endurance, grievous situations that are humanly absurd.

There are also harrowing trials that go on for months and years at a time, almost without respite, that take one's breath away. It's understandable why people complain and are tempted to rebel.

The truth is that pain is repulsive to our human nature.

So what should we do? Do we advise people to lessen their love for Jesus Forsaken, or even to renounce their preference for him and take back into their hearts other ideals, as for example—if that were even possible—happiness procured illicitly and at a small price? No. We have to encourage them to remain faithful to Jesus Forsaken at any cost, to remain faithful, because in the end he will be the source of their true happiness.

Jesus doesn't intend that we have nothing but suffering in life. He speaks also of the fullness of joy that we reach precisely through embracing Jesus Forsaken. [...]

So we must always take courage and renew our choice of him forsaken, repeating every morning, "Because you are forsaken," meaning that he is the motive force of our life. [...]

Let's go ahead this way.

We'll overcome the trials [...] in which we find ourselves and will be prepared to face the new ones.

Yes, because the whole of life can be seen as a long trial, and it does feel rather like that when one is under the lash of pain. But God, who is love, always alternates pain and joy, the Forsaken Christ with the Risen Christ.

If that's how it is, let's go ahead with courage, and also with hope. [...]

Remember: In whatever situation we find ourselves, let Jesus Forsaken be our one and only guiding star.

Revive our relationships

From an international conference call

Rocca di Papa, Italy, May 26, 1988[178]

Sanctity. But what is sanctity? The Church confirms it in Christians who have been found to have heroic virtues.

We, too, surely put no limit on the virtues we want to practice, yet when we hear talk about heroic virtues and make a brief examination of our lives, we cannot deny that we fall far short.

Which of us, looking back on our life, can say before God that we have had heroic patience, or heroic humility, fortitude, obedience, poverty or charity? Despite our good intentions, there always are and will be defects, imperfections, faults and offences that are difficult to eliminate.

With sorrow, therefore, we come to the conclusion that we are never going to reach sanctity. This situation could discourage us. What should we think?

First, we have to remember that reaching sanctity depends much more on God than on us. So we should never cease asking him for it as his gift. If we are assailed by the doubt of never making it to the end, or worse, if we feel this failure as one of the greatest, if not the greatest, failure in life, then we have to see, in this immense emptiness, the face of Jesus Forsaken. We have to welcome him, and await with faith the surprise of being totally filled with him.

We can also remember the laborer of the last hour; he gets the same reward as the one of the first hour. Therefore, we can always start all over again in earnest (cf. Mt 20:12).

But how? What does one aim at?

Since we have become aware, once again, that the only thing that counts is God and to love him as he deserves to be loved, and since we don't know how much time we have left in this life, we have to make the resolution to live the moment we have in our hands so well that we *are* the living Ideal.

There is a part of the Gospel that finds an echo in our hearts, and tells us what we have to do. Jesus says, "If you keep my commandments, you will abide in my love (...). *This* is my commandment, that you love one another" (Jn 15:10,12).

Consequently, everything depends on mutual love. [...]

This is the way we will truly love God and *be* the living Ideal! Charity lived in this way (and this is our hope) will generate solid virtues in us, and, almost without our noticing it, they will, with the grace of God, measure up to heroism. Living in this way, we will become saints.

So that the Risen Lord will shine out more and more

From an international conference call

Rocca di Papa, Italy, October 25, 1990[179]
We always need to remember that we have given our life to one alone, to Jesus Forsaken. Therefore, we cannot, and we should not, betray him or trade him off for something else.

He teaches us the immense value of suffering for the sake of unity. It is exactly through his cross, through his abandonment that he reunited human beings to God and to one another.

He is there on the cross, therefore, to tell us that unity has a cost, even though with him, and being like him, it can be achieved.

And so, if we want to be faithful to the charism of unity, which the Holy Spirit gave us, we need to once again throw open the doors of our heart to Jesus Forsaken and give him the best place.

Let's do it with infinite love, with gratitude, with determination and courage. He has been so close to us in life. He has to continue being there, now and forever. Let's propose to die rather than not love him forsaken.

During this month, to underline a concrete aspect of this love, let's love him in the difficulties that come in the effort to have unity among us [...].

We know that unity [...] in our various communities is not something that happens once and for all. It has to be built and rebuilt every day, and we can do it by loving the suffering that an imperfect unity (which is always possible) entails.

This means that we have to be always ready to see one another as "new," to be patient, to put up with one another, to know how to overlook things. It means to trust the other, to always hope, to always believe. And above all, it means not to judge. Judgement towards others, especially towards those in authority, is terrible; it is the opening through which the devil of disunity can enter. When judgement enters, every good of the soul slowly dissolves and one's vocation can even falter.

Therefore, let's concentrate on loving our brothers and sisters, with all the painful nuances this might entail, as the concrete proof of our decision to be ready to die for one another. This requires that we overcome the small or big obstacles out of love for Jesus Forsaken, so that our unity may always be full. Then the Risen Lord will always be alive and resplendent in our midst.

Chapter 6

"Jesus Forsaken and the Nights" Asceticism and mysticism in the Church and in society

A glance at history tells us that the lives of those great people who opened new paths for the life of the Church (and often also for the life of society), are generally characterized by extraordinary gifts of light with surprising effects, but also with striking tribulations.

Following Jesus Forsaken and making him the Ideal of her life meant that, in various moments and with increasing intensity, Chiara experienced a "dark night," which was always a prelude to new fruits. What emerged from her experience was the dynamics of both an asceticism and a mysticism that are not only personal, but also ecclesial and social. If this experience of Chiara is, on the one hand, unique and unrepeatable, on the other hand, it has charted a spiritual course of particular importance for our time. This is a topic which is very deep and beyond the context of this book, but which needs to be mentioned at least in brief.

1. "Different Seasons"

In every life there are alternating periods of light, enthusiasm and joy, with moments of pain, suffering and darkness. The more one goes forward, the more God purifies and sanctifies the person in all their dimensions, so that, like the branch of the vine that has been pruned, they may bear even more fruit. It is a more "passive" journey, but at the same time, it requires personal adherence and a progressively generous "yes," without reservations. Those who are committed to a Gospel-based way of life may see themselves in the following passages.

If fidelity is constant

From a page of her diary

January 2, 1979[180]

When I said, "I have only one Spouse on earth," [181] it was a declaration of love.

But when there are certain trails, one feels incapable of repeating those words. It is no longer the time or the season.

And yet, you realize that you have the grace to be faithful *moment by moment* (the only way possible) to that declaration that included every suffering.

Just like in our human life, the spiritual life has its different seasons and its different moments.

And if we are constantly faithful, the fruits come, the "children" are generated.

Yes, Jesus, you never deceived us.

It wasn't me who said and wrote, "I have only one Spouse…" It was you in me who pronounced those words.

Trials that threaten to crush us

From a page of her diary

February 27, 1981[182]

At times the "permitted" will [of God] allows us to go through trials that threaten to crush us, that throw us into deep anguish or at least give us great fear. […] It is the moment to remember that we have to accept only the anxiety of today, that tomorrow will have a grace of its own and surprises of God's love. We need to remember that God only asks us to love him, to embrace him forsaken now […] and that these are the days that have most value in his eyes. He sends these trials to us so that we grow strong in virtue and so that we make up for the days we didn't live so well.

Jesus wants us to be happy and at peace and he gave us the way: Jesus Forsaken. However, we shouldn't love him so as to gain something for ourselves […] but only for himself.

Like at the beginning: God alone

From a page of her diary

October 28, 1999[183]

I was attracted to the idea of finishing life as I started it: with God alone.

Now I think that it will indeed be like that, but with one variant. I want to finish my life as the spouse of Jesus Forsaken. With him, I will accomplish *unity*, that one and only idea that I have to pursue in order to become a saint.

In fact, with him I will always be united to God beyond every trail, and united with everyone else, especially those who most reflect his Face.

Thus I will also make the effort to "improve" every day, but along *this* line. (Whoever doesn't go forward goes backward.)

When I pass on to the next life, may they be able to say, "She was truly a spouse of Jesus Forsaken."

2. Four Nights

In 2006, in a time of great trial, Chiara dedicated important pages to "Jesus Forsaken and the nights." In her notes, collected in two themes, she first dwells, albeit briefly, on the night of the senses and the night of the spirit, which characterize primarily an individual spiritual path, as was outlined in particular by St. John of the Cross. She then explains how the "way of unity," which is ecclesial, individual and collective together, highlights also other facets of the "night," which had not yet been formulated: the "night of God" and the "collective and cultural night." All this is but one side of the paschal mystery of death and resurrection in which we are participants in Jesus, and is, therefore, the foundation of an increasingly amazing experience of the Risen Lord and his Spirit's action in our personal lives and in society.

Asceticism and mysticism in Christ Crucified and Risen

For centuries, the mystical aspect of Christian life was considered to be an exceptional event, confined mostly to the consecrated religious life and accompanied by particular phenomena such as ecstasies and visions. During the twentieth century, there was a growing awareness that Christian life as such has, or can have, a mystical dimension. We can all experience the presence of God and penetrate into his mystery with our lives, so that it may shape our actions. It is a mysticism of the people, which is lived in daily life, in the most diverse situations. The theologian Karl Rahner, grasping the importance and urgency of this development, had occasion to remark that the Christian of the future will either be a mystic or will not exist at all.[184]

From the text entitled "Jesus Forsaken and the four nights—Part 1" [185]

Many people realize that our lifestyle has a mystical dimension. I would actually say that it is a mystical way. This is manifested in various ways, depending on whether we are considering the night of the senses, or of the spirit, or the night of God.

Our spirituality clarifies the fact that the true Jesus Forsaken, whom we love, is very much joined to the sentence, "Father, into your hands I commend my spirit" (Lk 23:46)

Jesus Forsaken and the Risen Jesus are totally one with the realities of asceticism and mysticism. Here it is necessary to note that Jesus in his abandonment asked a question that requires an answer: the resurrection.

In fact, in suffering we see the ascetical effort, and in the light that comes from embracing it, the mystical aspect. [...]

Living our ideal, in whatever kind of "night" we experience, we are always in this double state of soul and what makes this possible is our relationship with Jesus Forsaken. He is the Master of both the ascetic aspect and the mystical aspect.

Night of the senses and night of the spirit

In an itinerary that is individual and collective at the same time, the experience of the "night of the senses" and the "night of the spirit," which according to St. John of the Cross mark the way to union with God, takes on new meaning.

From the text entitled "Jesus Forsaken and the four nights—Part 1" [186]

They are called "nights" because that's what they are like.

The first night involves, in general, our senses, our humanity. You may experience a long illness, or the loss of loved one, or undergo big failures, like economic collapse, and so on.

The second night is the night of the spirit, which was experienced, for the most part, by all the saints who were mystics.

In the following section, I have availed myself of definitions from the very valuable *Dictionary on Mysticism*, since it is a renowned publication. [187]

It states that a "night" is "a prolonged and profound spiritual experience, characterized by the sensation of aridity, obscurity and emptiness, lived and accepted as the absence of God."

In the night of the spirit, the person experiences a "total loss of any support 'like someone hanging in the air with nothing to lean on,' without present, past or future." [...]

Then another aspect of it is even more painful.

In the night of the spirit "the person doesn't only 'feel' aridity, darkness, torment, or misery, sin, impotence, but also 'believes' and interprets this as

God being angry with them, punishing and abandoning them with reason. The person 'believes that they are so full of evil that they merit to be abhorred by God and for good reason banished forever by God.'" [188] [...]

"This terrible burden and interior emptiness originates from, and is often accompanied by, distressing external circumstances, like tribulations, darkness, failures, persecutions, temptations."

"That which the person feels to be abandonment and even punishment is, in reality, a clear gesture of divine love and power. 'God teaches the soul and instructs it in the perfection of love, without the soul doing anything nor understanding how this is coming about.'" [189] [...]

"God illuminates and purifies the soul in a passive way through 'infused contemplation,' divine light that enlightens and dazzles, irritates the soul because of its immense bright light and because of the fragility of the soul. It makes the soul live and act with new motives and criteria that it does not comprehend." [...]

What is the difference between the night of the senses and the night of the spirit, and ourselves?

The difference between a movement with a collective spirituality and a movement with a more individualistic spirituality is that the first begins the journey together with friends while the second involves people who go to God alone.

We begin not by ourselves, but together with others. We journey ahead together with others. We scale the mountain towards God with Jesus in our midst. We are already in Christ. So we walk along the ridge of the mountain because Jesus in our midst can only be on the top. And that's why we go along the ridge. We don't climb up a path, but instead reach the top of the mountain immediately.

The trials are the same as all the others have, but we have the advantage (and also the disadvantage) of journeying together.

If the trials are sometimes softened, it's because they are lived with the help of Jesus in the midst, of Jesus in us and Jesus in our brother or sister.

The night of God

The following passage speaks of the dynamics of living a spirituality of communion, or rather, of living as a mystical body, where individuals are fused into one and live their particularity as an expression of this unity (cf. Gal 3:28 and Jn 17:21) and as a gift for others (cf. 1 Cor 12). It is, therefore, necessary to be "empty," figuratively speaking, before the other person, to set aside everything out of love, including our own personal union with God, to find, in mutual self-giving, the hundredfold promised by Jesus. It is a journey of "death" and "resurrection" that takes place in interpersonal relationships.

From the text entitled "Jesus Forsaken and the four nights—Part 1" [190]

But there is a third night that is typically ours. It is the night of God.

On April 3, 1950, I wrote: "St. John of the Cross, who is the master of nothingness, teaches us that everything has to be annihilated in us so that God can enter. That is the meaning of his night of the senses and of the spirit.

God asks something more of us [...]: he silences the senses, the intellect, the will, the memory and even the inspirations of God. [...]

Our life then is Jesus Forsaken. You live, like him, perfectly annihilated.

And this happens not only when many people come together and only one speaks. It happens always. When we speak with a brother or sister, we extinguish everything, even divine inspirations, in order to enter perfectly into that person, making ourselves nothing and therefore, simple. Only what is simple can enter everywhere. And that's what it means to be one. And thus we can see that being one is being Jesus Forsaken.

Collective and cultural night

With prophetic insight, John Paul II spoke of an "epochal dark night" in our times, and did not hesitate, at the opening of the third millennium, to refer to the cry of Jesus on the cross. Taking on this burden in all its various aspects, we find that love for Jesus Forsaken is the way to generate communion among people and within every sector of society. Thus we can give a powerful contribution to remove many obstacles and prepare the stage for a new moment in the life of humanity.

Talk prepared for the world meeting of the "Volunteers of God" on the 50th anniversary of their birth

Budapest, Hungary, September 16, 2006[191]

John Paul II did not hesitate to draw a parallel between the "dark night" of St. John of the Cross and the darkness of our times, which represents a sort of collective "night" into which humanity continues to fall, especially in the West.[192] [...]

It's clear to everyone that we need strong ideas, an ideal that opens a way that can give an answer to the numerous anguished questions of our day, a light to be followed, all the way to the point of saying with St. Laurence, "My night has no darkness, but all things break forth in light." [193]

In his apostolic letter, *At the beginning of the new millennium,* John Paul II announced a new star on our journey: Jesus Crucified and Forsaken. He said, "We shall never exhaust the depths of this mystery [...] "My God, my God, why have you forsaken me?" (Mk 15:34)[194]

Jesus Forsaken is presented, therefore, to the whole Church, at the suggestion of John Paul II, but he is not the only one to do so. Some of the saints of centuries ago and a few modern theologians had already offered him to Christianity. And then there is our movement, in which Jesus Forsaken is central.

This is exactly what we want to propose today: Jesus who cried out, "My God, my God, why have you forsaken me?"

It was his inner passion, his darkest night, the peak and culmination of his suffering. It is the drama of God who cries out, "My God, my God, why have you forsaken me?"

It is an infinite mystery, an unfathomable suffering that Jesus experienced as man, and that shows the measure of his love for humanity, since he wanted to take upon himself the separation that kept us far from the Father and from one another. He took it upon himself and filled it to the brim. [...]

Isn't he like a person who is in anguish, or alone, or spiritually dry, or disappointed, or a failure, or weak...? Isn't he the image of every painful separation among brothers and sisters, among churches, among large sections of humanity with contrasting ideologies? Isn't Jesus, who lost, so to say, the sense of God, who became "sin" for us (as Paul says), the symbol of the world that is against God, against the Church, plunged into every kind of abnormality?

Loving Jesus Forsaken we find the motivation and the strength to never flee from these evils, these divisions, but to accept them, consume them and give them our individual and collective remedy.

If we manage to meet him in every suffering, if we love him and repeat with Jesus on the cross, "Father, into your hands I commend my spirit" (Lk 23:46), the night will pass and we will find the light.

3. "Entering Into" Jesus Forsaken

We read in the Letter to the Colossians: "I am now rejoicing in my sufferings for your sake; and in my flesh I am completing what is lacking in Christ's afflictions for the sake of his body, that is, the church" (Col 1:24). Paul is obviously not speaking about adding something to the work of Christ, but rather about how it can impact humanity, through the life of Jesus in us. This type of trial is found in Chiara's spiritual path, just as in the life of others who witnessed to the Gospel. She made this experience over the years in an ever deeper way, until the last trial in the years 2004–2008, which, as she herself said, had the characteristics of a "complete darkening" for long periods of time. It is the culmination of a life spent unreservedly for unity, projected out towards others in the commitment to build bridges and fill the many gaps that so painfully divide individuals, peoples and cultures. It is her final offering for the fulfilment of the human family. Chiara's notes during 2006 speak of this unfathomable experience, during which she said: "I offer my sufferings for all the sinners of the world." [195]

From the text, "Jesus Forsaken and the four nights—Part 2" [196]

There is a second night of God that involves a total darkening of the soul. This is the trial that one lives at a certain point in life.

A new understanding of God opens up on a totally different level. It consists not only of the cry of Jesus Forsaken but also of every possible suffering, in particular in the spiritual realm. It is different from the night of the spirit, in which you at least feel that God is present and he is the one making you suffer.

You realize that this is another kind of night: the final "night" that one can experience here on earth.

What does it mean?

It means that God is extremely distant.

The soul feels alone, tormented by incredible sufferings. "To whom can I turn? Who can I lean on?" And yet in a particular way, one no longer feels God, in the sense that God has gone far away. He, too, goes out towards the far "horizon of the sea." We had followed him up to that point, but at the far edge of the sea, he disappears beyond the horizon, and one can no longer see him at all. At least this is how the person feels.

Therefore, while we had believed previously that the nights of the spirit ended by embracing Jesus Forsaken, we realize that in this instance we *enter into* Jesus Forsaken.

In his cry, Jesus in a certain way reproached the Father. In this kind of trial, the soul, in its immense sadness, is tempted to blame God. [...]

One really has to speak of "beyond the horizon," where God is no longer visible and the soul descends so far down into this night that it loses everything for months and months, everything, truly everything.

It's a terrible shock: God is no longer felt.

While up to the edge of the horizon, one could feel the pain, at this point, the person no longer feels God.

The soul is left alone.

The person is given the opportunity to understand up to what point God wants the soul stripped. One no longer believes, no longer loves, no longer remembers. One does not exist.

And the soul cries out, but faith does nothing for it. It asks for graces, but they are no longer there.

It truly does not exist. This is unbearable. [...]

It is a participation in being "Jesus Forsaken-similar to hell." In other words, God abandons you.[197]

You think: "God does not think about me, God does not remember me...." Why? Why? Almost as if the Father had made a mistake by abandoning you.

Some months later, Chiara wrote:

In those days, thinking of the grain of wheat that is destined to die, I felt dead in the "abandonment—hell." I could not imagine that any fruits could come from this.

Now instead, from what we can see, the fruits are beyond anything that we could have imagined.[198]

Epilogue
Jesus Forsaken and Unity

To young people who live the ideal of unity

February 1968[199]
Our motto, "That they may all be one," rests heavily on our shoulders. At the same time, however, it gives us great supernatural pride. It is something wonderful.

I believe that it would be impossible to think of words more beautiful and sublime than these. It causes us to dream of a world different from that which surrounds us. It stirs the imagination to wonder what society would be like if this great word of God were fulfilled.

Imagine a world where people loved one another and where everyone shared the same feelings. In this new world, prisons would disappear and policemen become obsolete. The dark news of daily papers would be replaced by "golden news," facts and stories which are divinely beautiful and deeply human. People would sing, play, study and work. Everything, however, would be done in complete harmony. Everyone would do only what pleases God and others.

I think we shall see such a world only in heaven.

But Jesus said, "That they may all be one" precisely for us here on earth. [...]

I opened the Gospel and found another sentence that seems to be similar to the first. A secret bond seems to exist between it and our motto. It says, "When I am lifted up from the earth, I will draw all people to myself." (Jn 12:32).

All people!

That "all" is also present in our motto, "That they may all be one."

Could this, then, be the way to fulfill it?

Did Jesus offer us the key to obtain it?

"When I am lifted up from the earth. . ." Jesus did not make us "all one" through beautiful words and extraordinary miracles...

The cross was Jesus' secret. It was his suffering that made us children of God and, therefore, all one.

Could suffering then be the way, the key, the secret of unity? Could it possess the secret that will transform this evil world into one of joy, love and paradise?

Yes.

From the little we know, we see that the saints, who are truly wise, have all given great value to suffering and the cross. They attracted a large number of followers, and often left their mark on history, with a beneficial influence also on subsequent centuries.

When I was a small child, a priest told me, "There is an empty place on the cross." Turning the crucifix around, he showed me the back of it and added, "This place must be occupied by you!"

Very well! If this is so, we're ready!

What are we waiting for?

In any case, suffering, both big or small, accepted well or badly, will always be a part of life...

But we don't want to exploit him! No, we are Christians! Jesus is on the cross and that's where I want to be.

I will accept all the little crosses in my life with joy. Yes, with joy, even though I might shed some tears. Nevertheless, deep down in my heart I will tell him who listens to me: "I am happy. By suffering with you, I can help in drawing all people to you. In this way we will be nearer to the day when your immense desire, 'That they may all be one,' will be fulfilled."

Endnotes

1 Chiara Lubich, *The Cry of Jesus Crucified and Forsaken*, (New York: New City Press, 2001), 61–62.

2 Chiara Lubich—Igino Giordani, *"Erano i tempi di guerra..."*, Città Nuova, Roma 2007, 27–32, our translation.

3 Chiara Lubich, *Jesus: The Heart of His Message, Unity and Jesus Forsaken*, (New York: New City Press, 1985), 46.

4 Ibid.

5 An adventure that the author describes in the book *The Cry*, whose topic is: Jesus Crucified and Forsaken in the history and life of the Focolare Movement, from its birth in 1943 until the dawn of the third millennium.

6 We refer mostly to Chiara Lubich, *Early Letters: At the origins of a new spirituality*, (New York: New City Press, 2012). Many of the letters that Chiara wrote to different people in those years have not been preserved. This explains the recurrence of some of the recipients of those letters.

7 *The Cry*, 36–37

8 *Jesus: The Heart of His Message*, 44.

9 *The Cry*, 38–39.

10 It's significant how much Chiara emphasizes the link between unity and Jesus Forsaken as the key to accomplish it. In the book, *Jesus: The Heart of His Message*, Chiara offers more details about this prayer which was made most probably on the feast of Christ the King either in 1944 or 1945. (cf. *Jesus: The Heart of His Message*, 23).

11 Chiara Lubich, *Early Letters: At the Origins of a New Spirituality*, (New York: New City Press, 2012), 16–17.

12 Ibid., 29–30.

13 In the letter there is first a description of the passionate love St. Catherine of Siena had for Jesus Crucified.

14 *Early Letters*, 22–25.

15 Letter to Fr. Raffaele Massimei, OFM Conv., June 15, 1948, in *Early Letters*, 113.

16 *Early Letters*, 27–28.

17 Ibid., 33–34.

18 Sylvia is the baptismal name of Chiara Lubich; she took the name "Chiara" when she became a member of the Third Order of St. Francis and then she kept it even afterwards.

19 *Early Letters*, 31–32.

20 Chiara Lubich Center Archives, unpublished, our translation.

21 Letter from April 23, 1948, to Fr. Raffaele Massimei, OFM Conv., in *Early Letters*, 102.

22 Chiara Lubich, *Essential Writings*, (New York: New City Press, 2007), 97.

23 *Gesú Abbandonato e la vita*, in "Gen's" 36 (2006), 6–7, our translation.

24 *Early Letters*, 49–50.

25 See Lk 23:46.

26 See Jn 17, 10.

27 See *Gesú Abbandonato e la vita,* 7–8, our translation.

28 Chiara Lubich, *Essential Writings*, (New York: New City Press, 2007), 94.

29 "Nuova Umanitá" 29 (2007) 170, 185, our translation.

30 The date on this text is the date it was printed in a duplicated publication entitled, *"48 hours of unity"* 2 (1957) 5, 5, our translation.

31 *Gesú Abbandonato e la vita*, 4–5, our translation.

32 Because of the allusion to superiors and to the small community, it is thought that this letter was probably written

to two Sisters, most likely Franciscans, in Rovereto, to whom Chiara had already written on October 3 (1946?) and October 14, 1946.

33 *Early Letters*, 79–80.

34 Ibid., 90.

35 Ibid., 92–93.

36 Ibid., 98–99.

37 Ibid., 101–102.

38 Ibid., 112–113.

39 See Col 3:1.

40 Chiara is referring to the moment in which, because of various difficulties, there was the possibility that the newborn movement would be disbanded.

41 See Mt 13:45.

42 See Ps 21:7.

43 See Song 3.

44 *Gesú Abbandonato e la vita*, 11, our translation.

45 The trial that Chiara referred to in the previous letter had passed and Archbishop Carlo De Ferrari confirmed his full support of the movement.

46 Chiara is referring to the archbishop of Trent, Carlo De Ferrari.

47 *Gesú Abbandonato e la vita*, 13, our translation.

48 See the story of the "Pact of Unity" in Chiara Lubich, *Unity* (New York: New City Press, 2015), 62–66.

49 The notes in chapter 2 are from the author unless otherwise indicated.

50 This expression is used in *The Cry*, (New York: New City Press, 2001), 111.

51 *Il Patto del '49 nell'esperienza di Chiara Lubich. Percorsi interdisciplinari*, Città Nuova, Roma 2012, 11–14, our translation.

52 Intensely living the Word, I had observed (...) that in it there is always a negative part—for example: "Blessed are the poor in spirit"—and a positive part—"for theirs is the kingdom of heaven" (Mt 5:3); even though it may seem that one of these two aspects is lacking, nonetheless that aspect is implicit. It seemed to me I understood that in every Word there is present Jesus, dead and risen: in the negative part of the Word is present and expressed the death of Jesus; in the positive, his resurrection. And, in fact, the very existence of Jesus, entirely lived out in total love for the Father and for human beings, was all death and resurrection: the expression and revelation on earth of the "non-being and being" of the love within the Trinity. The same reality therefore is in his Word, in each one of his Words. And the same reality is present and manifested in the existence of whoever lives the Word, and so in the life of the Church.

53 "Paradise '49," *Claritas, A Journal of Dialogue and Culture*, 1 (March 2012): 6–7. http://docs.lib.purdue.edu/claritas/vol1/iss1/3.

54 "Nuova Umanitá" 29 (2007) 170, 171, our translation.

55 Cf 2 Cor 5:21.

56 We often connect, even though not always explicitly, the cry of Jesus to others words of his, like, "Father, into your hands I commend my spirit" (Lk 23:46), which seem to express the same reality. In fact, for us it seems that Jesus Forsaken re-abandoned himself to the Father in an act of infinite love. That is why here I can write that he is "boldness."

57 Jesus and the Holy Spirit are always one (see 2 Cor 3:17); but where this unity is best seen is in the abandonment in which Jesus gives us the Holy Spirit. Thus, if we embrace Jesus Forsaken, we have the Holy Spirit.

58 "Nuova Umanitá" 20 (1998) 117/118, 397, our translation; 29 (2007) 170, 179, our translation.

59 I mean to say that there is no longer any emptiness on earth just as there is none in heaven.

60 2 Cor 5:21.

61 "Nuova Umanitá" 18 (1996) 103, 34, our translation.

62 "Nuova Umanitá" 29 (2007) 170, 182–183, our translation.

63 See 2 Cor 5:21. It is a grace to be able to make this act of pure love. It is necessary that one remembers Jesus Forsaken, who became "sin" for us, and embraces one's own state of sinfulness to be a little similar to him. It's necessary to prepare oneself to die well, starting right away, doing it as a pure act of love throughout our life so as to have the strength to do it at the end.

64 "Gen's" 36 (2006), 52, our translation.

65 We understood why Jesus Forsaken cried, screamed. It is like a mother who cries out when giving birth to her child, and he too cried out when he gave birth to the children of God. [Jesus himself used the image of the pains of childbirth when he said, "When a woman is in labour, she has pain, because her hour has come. But when her child is born, she no longer remembers the anguish because of the joy of having brought a human being into the world." (Jn. 16:21)]

66 Ed: to deepen this concept, see *The Cry*, 24–25.

67 Chiara Lubich Center Archives, unpublished, our translation.

68 "Nuova Umanitá" 24 (2002) 143, 584, our translation.

69 [...] I had understood that Jesus Forsaken was like a deep hole, a nothingness, and since he was nothingness, through him humanity could see God. I had also understood that Jesus Forsaken was the point through which God looked onto humanity, even though God always sees everything. However, it was through the redemption that he was in full contact with humanity and humanity had been placed in full contact with him. We were born from that wound, it was at that moment that we were generated. Therefore, it is in the abandonment of Jesus, in the moment when he was the Mediator, that God touches, so to speak, humanity. That was the moment of

contact and that is also the moment of contact of people with God.

70 "Nuova Umanitá" 22 (2000) 132, 779, our translation.

71 "Nuova Umanitá" 18 (1996) 103, 39, our translation.

72 What is asked is the detachment from our way of thinking, from thinking itself. This is the non-being of the mind. It's this that makes us like Jesus Forsaken. And this is true also for the will, the memory, the imagination. We reach these "deaths" above all by loving, making the will of God our own and loving others, but also by "losing" when we have the temptation to keep our will, our thoughts, etc.

73 We speak of the imagination, too, because, differently, we think, from other spiritualities, we underline the "beautiful." And also because unity is something more than loving your neighbor as yourself; unity is loving one another to the point of dying for one another. Unity, the fruit of mutual love is harmony, is beauty.

74 In other words, totally empty.

75 We can have this "infinite nothingness" by loving Jesus Forsaken not only in suffering, which is him, but also in joy, which we set aside for him, choosing him again as our one and only good.

76 "Nuova Umanitá" 20 (1998) 119, 548, our translation.

77 "Nuova Umanitá" 32 (2010) 187, 30, our translation.

78 It is through losing, losing, losing, and loving Jesus Forsaken that you reach the point of having only the Holy Spirit. Then he will be the one to suggest to you the answer to every question, the solution to every problem.

79 "Nuova Umanitá" 18 (1996) 105/106, 346, our translation.

80 "Nuova Umanitá" 32 (2010) 188, 196, our translation.

81 See Mt 22:37.

82 Editor's note: "To make the Church *the home and the school of communion*: that is the great challenge facing us

in the millennium which is now beginning, if we wish to be faithful to God's plan and respond to the world's deepest yearnings. But what does this mean in practice? [...] Before making practical plans, we need *to promote a spirituality of communion* (John Paul II, *At the beginning of the New Millennium*, 43). "Today, when the networks and means of human communication have made unprecedented advances, we sense the challenge of finding and sharing a 'mystique' of living together, of mingling and encounter, of embracing and supporting one another, of stepping into this flood tide which, while chaotic, can become a genuine experience of fraternity, a caravan of solidarity, a sacred pilgrimage." (Pope Francis, *The Joy of the Gospel*, 87; 92 and 72). Benedict XVI used mostly the language of friendship and fraternity.

83 Chiara Lubich, *Guardare tutti i fiori. Da una pagina del '49 di Chiara Lubich*, Città Nuova, Roma 2014, 35, our translation.

84 This page is very important in order to put into practice our "making ourselves one with everyone." "We need to be nothing (Jesus Forsaken) in front of every person" and not have any preoccupation about communicating to them something about our Ideal. One communicates by being nothing. This is the way of our inculturation: "everyone can write on nothing." In these pages we find the Ideal with which we always need to compare ourselves, so that we love not only our own movement, not only our own Church, but also the other churches; not only the "militant church on earth" [Christians who are still living and struggling on earth], but also the triumphant church in heaven and those in purgatory, and all the other, believers and non-believers. This is what we must become. It is the patrimony that I leave you for the future, so that there will always be people who live like this.

85 Mt 25:40.

86 See Mt 25:31–46; Jn 5:24; 1 Cor 6:1–3.

87 Chiara Lubich, *L'amore al fratello*, F. Gillet (ed.), Città Nuova, Roma 2011, 29, our translation.

88 This vision of our neighbor is stupendous. If we love others, we find union with God; otherwise, we do not.

89 "Nuova Umanitá" 32 (2010) 188, 201, our translation.

90 "Nuova Umanitá" 19 (1997) 111/112, 402, our translation.

91 *Scritti spirituali/1*, Città Nuova, Roma 1991, 35, our translation.

92 "Nuova Umanitá" 20 (1998) 119, 510, our translation.

93 "Nuova Umanitá" 35 (2013) 206, 172–173, our translation.

94 *Scritti spirituali/1*, Città Nuova, Roma 1991, 42, our translation.

95 Ibid.

96 See *The Cry*, 71.

97 Chiara Lubich, *Frammenti, Città Nuova, Roma 1963*, reprinted in: *Scritti spirituali/1*, 232–235, our translation.

98 See Heb 9:22.

99 See *Early Letters*, 128.

100 Chiara Lubich Center Archives, unpublished, our translation.

101 Ibid.

102 Ibid.

103 See *The Cry*, 68.

104 Ibid., 66.

105 In an answer to young people in formation for life in the focolare households, on June 22, 1981, in Loppiano (Florence), Chiara spoke of three things that were learned from that period: the awareness that we never build anything without suffering; the certainty that suffering is necessary to purify us and help us mature; and the realization that suffering makes a work of God grow, but also allows us to collaborate with Jesus in bringing about the redemption.

106 See *The Cry*, 67; 71–72; 85.

107 Ibid., 75; 77–82.

108 Ibid., 75–76.

109 The mysterious spiritual wound in the heart of Jesus Forsaken.

110 Chiara Lubich Center Archives, unpublished, our translation.

111 See *The Cry*, 88–89.

112 See *Essential Writings*, 56–57.

113 See *The Cry*, 83–84.

114 See *Essential Writings*, 150–151.

115 Chiara Lubich, *Scritti spirituali/3*, Città Nuova, Roma 1996, 54, our translation.

116 This is how Chiara defines Jesus Forsaken in her *Lectio magistralis* at the ceremonies when she received honorary doctorates in theology in Manila and in philosophy in Mexico City. See *Essential Writings*, New City Press, New York, 2007, 201–214.

117 Chiara Lubich, *Pensieri* (1961), published in *Scritti spirituali/1*, 135, our translation.

118 *Santi insieme*, Città Nuova, Roma 1994, 79, our translation.

119 *Scritti spirituali/3*, Città Nuova, Roma 1996, 51, our translation.

120 *Le sfide sociali e i religiosi*, F. Ciardi (ed.), Città Nuova, Roma 1995, 41–43, our translation.

121 See Mt 25: 40.

122 *Colloqui con i gen. Anni 1975–2000*, Città Nuova, Roma 2001, 48–50, our translation.

123 *Colloqui con i gen. Anni 1970–1974*, Città Nuova, Roma 1999, 73–83, our translation.

124 See *The Cry*, 105–111.

125 *The Cry*, 105–106.

126 P. Coda—B. Leahy (edd.), *Preti in un mondo che cambia*, Città Nuova, Roma 2010, 19–20, 28, our translation.

127 See R. Guardini, *Il Signore*, Università Cattolica, Milano 1964, 493–494.

128 See Giovanni della Croce, *Salita del Monte Carmelo*, 2, 7, 11, in: *Opere*, Roma 1979.

129 *Gesù abbandonato: via maestra per una comunità in dialogo*, in «Gen's» 32 (2002), 109, our translation.

130 See *The Cry,* 114.

131 See *Preti in un mondo che cambia,* 24–25, our translation.

132 This is the name given by the Church when the Focolare Movement was officially approved.

133 Chiara Lubich Center Archives, unpublished, our translation.

134 See *The Cry*, 114–115.

135 *Dove la vita si accende*, Città Nuova, Roma 1998, 22–23, our translation.

136 *Una famiglia per rinnovare la società*, Città Nuova, Roma 1993, 116, 119–120, our translation.

137 "Nuova Umanitá" 21 (1999) 125, 482–484, our translation.

138 See *The Cry*, 136.

139 Cf. Chiara Lubich Center in collaboration with the Sophia Institute, *Doctorate honoris causa* conferred on Chiara Lubich.

140 See *Essential Writings*, 221–222.

141 Ibid., 313–314.

142 John Paul II, *To the artists,* May 20, 1985.

143 *Essential Writings*, 294–295.

144 Cf. G.M. Zanghí, *Some comments about Jesus Forsaken*, in "Nuova Umanitá" 19 (1996) 103, 37.

145 Chiara Lubich Center Archives, unpublished, our translation.

146 *Gesù abbandonato e la vita*, 4, our translation.

147 Chiara Lubich Center Archives, unpublished, our translation.

148 Ibid.

149 Ibid.

150 Ibid.

151 Chiara Lubich, *Journey: Spiritual Insights*, (New York: New City Press, 1984), 53–54.

152 Chiara Lubich Center Archives, unpublished, our translation.

153 Ibid.

154 Ibid.

155 Ibid.

156 Ibid.

157 On the occasion of her trip to Australia, Chiara took the example of the kangaroo, which can only jump forward, as a model for the determination needed to pass from one will of God to another, without hesitating and without attachments.

158 *Journey: Spiritual Insights*, 53.

159 Ibid., 22.

160 Chiara Lubich Center Archives, unpublished, our translation.

161 *Journey: Spiritual Insights,* 126–127.

162 Igino Giordani (1894–1980), member of parliament and of the constituent Assembly, highly regarded personage in the civil and ecclesiastical society, an author and a journalist. He met Chiara Lubich in 1948 and later became the first married focolarino. The cause of his beatification is in process.

163 Cf Igino Giordani, *Diary of Fire,* (New York: New City Press, 1981),43.

164 The "volunteers of God" are people who are committed to living the Ideal of unity and giving witness to it wherever they are, in particular in their workplace and professional life, with the goal of renewing society and bringing about universal brotherhood.

165 Chiara Lubich Center Archives, unpublished, our translation.

166 *Journey: Spiritual Insights,* 134–135.

167 Chiara Lubich Center Archives, unpublished, our translation.

168 Ibid.

169 Ibid.

170 *Journey: Spiritual Insights,* 85–86.

171 Chiara Lubich Center Archives, unpublished, our translation.

172 Ibid.

173 Chiara Lubich, *On the Holy Journey,* (New York: New City Press, 1988), 97–98.

174 Ibid., 142–143.

175 Chiara Lubich, *Journey to Heaven: Spiritual Thoughts to Live,* (New York: New City Press, 1997), 33–35.

176 This verse is found only in the Douay-Rheims (DRA) version of the Bible, 1899.

177 *Journey to Heaven,* 52–54.

178 Ibid., 94–96.

179 *Santi insieme,* 53–54, our translation.

180 Chiara Lubich Center Archives, unpublished, our translation.

181 Chiara refers to the declaration of love that burst spontaneously from her heart on September 20, 1949, and that remained as a constant reference point for her life.

182 *La volontà di Dio,* L. Abignente (ed.), Città Nuova, Roma 2011, 97, our translation.

183 Chiara Lubich Center Archives, unpublished, our translation.

184 Cf. *Nuovi saggi*, vol. 2, San Paolo, Roma 1968, 24, our translation.

185 Chiara Lubich Center Archives, unpublished, our translation.

186 Ibid.

187 The quotes are translated from F. Ruiz, *Notte oscura*, in *Dizionario di Mistica*, di L. Borriello—E. Caruana—M.R. Del Genio—N. Suffi (edd.), Libreria Editrice Vaticana, Città del Vaticano 1998, 913–916. The author goes back to expressions and quotes of St. John of the Cross.

188 St. John of the Cross, *The dark night* II, 7, 7.

189 *Ibid.*, II, 5, 1.

190 Chiara Lubich Center Archives, unpublished, our translation.

191 Ibid.

192 Cf. John Paul II, *Homily on the occasion of the celebration for St. John of the Cross*, Segovia, November 4, 1982; *Talk to the Carmelite General Chapter*, Rome, September 29, 1989.

193 St. Laurence, a Roman deacon, who died as a martyr in the year 258 said [in Latin]: *"Mea nox obscurum non habet, sed omnia in luce clarescunt."* ["My night has no darkness, but all things break forth into light."]

194 John Paul II, *Novo millennio ineunte*, 25.

195 "Nuova Umanità" 31 (2009) 182, 187, our translation.

196 "Nuova Umanità" 32 (2010) 189, 372–373, our translation.

197 In the trial God distances himself and Jesus Forsaken gives us an intuition of what hell might be like.

198 Chiara was reading the reports on the life and activities of the movement throughout the world.

199 Chiara Lubich, *The Gen Revolution*, (Manila: New City Press, 1972), 46–49.

About Chiara Lubich

Chiara Lubich (1920-2008) was founder of the Focolare Movement (The Work of Mary). Born in Trent, Italy, her baptismal name was Silvia. In 1943, when she entered the Third Franciscan Order, she took the name Chiara because she was attracted by St. Clare of Assisi's radical choice of God. 1943 also marks the year that Chiara Lubich made a vow of chastity, and it has become the year associated with the birth of the Focolare. In the course of her life, she saw the spirituality of the Focolare – the spirituality of unity – grow around the world. She was awarded 15 honorary doctoral degrees, numerous civic awards, the Templeton Prize for Progress of Religion, and the UNESCO Peace Prize. She has published more than 50 books in 29 languages.

Today, the Focolare Movement that she founded is present in 182 countries. It has approximately 2 million adherents and people who are sympathetic to its goals – the majority being Roman Catholic. There is a growing number of non-Catholics from 350 churches and ecclesial communities. The movement also includes many from other world faiths for example Jews, Muslims, Buddhists, Hindus and Sikhs. Then there are also those in the movement who do not adhere to any particular religious faith.

The following titles are based on the thought and experience of Chiara Lubich.

Biography

A Woman's Work: Story of the Focolare Movement and Its Founder, Jim Gallagher 1998, 978-1-56548-099-5, $12.95
Chiara Lubich: A Biography, Armando Torno, 2012, 978-1-56548-453-5, e * $14.95

Economy and Work

Structures of Grace, The Business Practices of the Economy of Communion, John Gallagher & Jeanne Buckeye, 2014, 978-1-56548-551-8, e $14.95

Ecumenical and Interreligious Dialogue

5 Steps to Living Christian Unity: Insights & Examples, Callan Slipper, 2013, 978-1-56548-501-3, e $4.95
5 Steps to Positive Political Dialogue: Insights & Examples, Amy Uelmen, 2014, 978-1-56548-507-5, $4.95
A Dialogue of Life, Towards the Encounter of Jews and Christians, Chemen/Canzani, 2015, 978-1-56548-562-4, e $14.95
A Handbook of Spiritual Ecumenism, A Tool for Applied Ecumenism, Cardinal Walter Kasper, 2014, 978-1-56548-263-0, $9.95

Family Life

5 Steps to Building Unity in a Marriage: Insights & Examples, Kevin & Katie Kelly, 2015, 978-1-56548-512-9, e $4.95
5 Steps to Effective Student Leadership: Insights & Examples, Carr/James/Trost, 2014, 978-1-56548-509-9, e $4.95
Education's Highest Aim: Teaching and Learning through a Spirituality of Communion, James/Masters/Uelmen, 2010, 978-1-56548-336-1, $14.95
Gifts from Heaven: Providence in Our Family, Tom & Mary A. Hartmann, 2012, 978-1-56548-429-0, e $11.95
John of the Smiles, The Story of a Boy whose Light Transformed People around Him, Geraldine Guadagno, 2016, 978-1-56548-600-3, $15.95

---

* e indicates that an e-book version is available

Thriving Marriages, An Inspirational and Practical Guide to Lasting Happiness, John Yzaguirre & Claire-Frazier Yzaguirre, 2015, 978-1-56548-591-4, e $14.95

God is Love

God Who Is Love, in the Experience and Thought of Chiara Lubich, Marisa Cerini, 2005, 978-1-56548-004-9, $9.95

Jesus Forsaken

15 Days of Prayer with Blessed Chiara Badano, Florence Gillet, 2015, 978-1-56548-554-9, e $13.95

5 Steps to Facing Suffering: Insights & Examples, Geraldine Guadagno, 2014, 978-1-56548-502-0, e $4.95

Chiara Badano DVD, A Teen's Life and Beatification, Maria A. Calò, 2011, 978-1-56548-424-5, $15.95

Chiara Luce: Life Lived to the Full, Michele Zanzucchi, 2008, 978-1-56548-798-1, $9.95

Jesus Forsaken, in the Experience and Thought of Chiara Lubich, Hubertus Blaumeister, 2016, 978-1-56548-613-3, $15.95

Jesus: The Heart Of His Message, Unity and Jesus Forsaken, Chiara Lubich, 1985, 978-1-56548-090-2, $8.95

The Choice of Jesus Forsaken in the Theological Perspective of Chiara Lubich, Florence Gillet, 2015, 978-1-56548-506-8, e $13.95

The Cry of Jesus Crucified and Forsaken, Chiara Lubich, 2001, 978-1-56548-159-6, $11.95

Where Is God In Suffering? Reconciling Faith in God in Today's World, Fr. Brendan Purcell, 2016, 978-1-56548-621-8, $15.95

Mary

Mary: The Transparency of God, Chiara Lubich, 2003, 978-1-56548-192-3, e $11.95

Spirituality of Unity

15 Days of Prayer with Chiara Lubich, Florence Gillet, 2015, 978-1-56548-513-6, e $13.95

A New Way, The Spirituality of Unity, Chiara Lubich, 2006, 978-1-56548-236-4, $12.95

Chiara Lubich's Communitarian Way to Holiness in the Light of John 17:11b-19, Paloma Cabetas, 2015, 978-1-56548-581-5, e $5.95

Focolare: Living a Spirituality of Unity in the United States, Tom Masters & Amy Uelmen, 2011, 978-1-56548-374-3, e $16.95

Introduction to the Abba School, Conversations from the Focolare's Interdisciplinary Study Center, various authors, 2002, 978-1-56548-176-3, e $11.95

The Art of Loving, A handbook to Answer the Call to Love, Chiara Lubich, 2010, 978-1-56548-335-4, $11.95

The Trinity: Life of God, Hope for Humanity: Towards a Theology of Communion (Theology and Faith), Fr. Thomas Norris, 2009, 978-1-56548-312-4, $17.95

Theses for a Trinitarian Ontology by Bishop Klaus Hemmerle, translated by Tom Norris, 2016, 978-1-56548-620-1, $13.95

Trinity: Model of Society, Enrique Cambon, 2017, 978-1-56548-477-1, $24.95

The Eucharist

Eucharist—Four Talks of Chiara Lubich, Chiara Lubich, 2005, 978-1-56548-224-1, e $7.95

His Mass and Ours: Meditations on Living Eucharistically, Brendan Leahy, 2012, 978-1-56548-448-1, e $7.95

Jesus Eucharist, in the Experience and Thought of Chiara Lubich, Fabio Ciardi, 2016, 978-1-56548-580-8, $12.95

Unity

Unity, in the Experience and Thought of Chiara Lubich, Chiara Lubich, 2015, 978-1-56548-593-8, e $14.95

Writings

Chiara Lubich, Essential Writings: Spirituality Dialogue Culture, Michel Vandeleene, 2007, 978-1-56548-259-3, e $24.95

Early Letters: At the Origins of a New Spirituality, Chiara Lubich, 2012, 978-1-56548-432-0, e $15.95

New City Press

of the Focolare

Hyde Park, New York

New City Press is one of more than 20 publishing houses sponsored by the Focolare, an ecclesial movement founded by Chiara Lubich to help bring about the realization of Jesus' prayer: "That all may be one" (John 17:21). In view of that goal, New City Press publishes books and resources that enrich the lives of people and help all to strive toward the unity of the entire human family. We are a member of the Association of Catholic Publishers.

www.NewCityPress.com

 Scan to join our mailing list for discounts and promotions

Periodicals
Living City Magazine, www.livingcitymagazine.com